George Butterworth
Soldier and Composer

To Gerry Barratt, wherever you are.

LAURENCE GREEN

GEORGE BUTTERWORTH
SOLDIER AND COMPOSER

Published in 2018 by Fighting High Ltd,
www.fightinghigh.com

Copyright © Fighting High Ltd, 2018
Copyright text © Laurence Green, 2018

British Library Cataloguing-in-Publication data.
A CIP record for this title is available from the
British Library.

ISBN – 13: 978-1999812805

Designed and typeset in Adobe Minion 11/15pt
by Michael Lindley, www.truthstudio.co.uk.

Printed and bound in Wales by Gomer Press.
Front cover design by www.truthstudio.co.uk.

Contents

Introduction   VII

Part One – Composer
1. Deerhurst   1
2. Aysgarth   7
3. Eton   14
4. Oxford   25
5. *The Times*, Radley College and The Royal College of Music   37

Part Two – Army Officer
6. Light Infantry   60
7. Hampstead and back to France   90
8. The Somme   105
9. Bailiff Wood: 7 July 1916   112
10. Bailiff Wood: 8 July 1916   116
11. Bailiff Wood: 9 July 1916   119
12. Bailiff Wood and Contalmaison: 10 July 1916   123
13. Albert: 11 to 15 July 1916   126
14. 17 to 25 July 1916   131
15. 26 July 1916   135
16. 1 to 5 August 1916   140
17. One Hundred Years Later   148

Acknowledgements and Bibliography   158
Index   160

Introduction

George Butterworth was an enigmatic man. Intense, single-minded and often unapproachable, he made few friends but kept those to whom he was close until the end of his all too short life. He was a loyal friend, a composer of exceptional talent, and a very competent Army officer, all in the space of thirty-one years. For most of his life he was undecided about how to earn his living. Few composers could make a good income by their composition alone. There was always a tension between what Butterworth knew he must do to satisify his soul and what he felt he should do in order to support himself financially. That tension was resolved by the coming of the Great War and the call of duty to fight for an England that was his muse and his inspiration.

He was very much a man of his time and yet his music has transcended the time in which it was written. As I write this piece it is the evening of the last night of the Proms. Second on the programme is Butterworth's *The Banks of Green Willow*. Last weekend our village pub staged a beer festival that involved as its centrepiece the local morris-dancing side. Had it not been for Butterworth and his friends, morris dancing might have continued to decline into oblivion in the rural shires of England.

Butterworth's relevance is timeless. Even as he wrote his beautiful songs and orchestral pieces based firmly in the English countryside, that very countryside was changing. The drift from the land, increasing mechanisation in farming and industrial unrest in the growing towns was threatening the equilibrium of England. The clouds of war were gathering across the Channel. As Mrs Bunch, the housekeeper in M.R. James's terrifying ghost story *Lost Hearts*, says: 'They're a hunruly lot, them foreign nations, I do suppose.'

The years leading up to the Great War were not timeless fine summer days. They were not A.E. Housman's *Land of Lost Content*, but were a struggle for nearly everybody, including George Butterworth. The war came as a catharsis for some, oblivion for the nearly ten per cent of men who 'would never grow old'. Unfortunately, this included Butterworth. All was not lost, though. Most of the English countryside that Butterworth loved and enjoyed still exists. Many of the traditions he helped to preserve are alive and well and are thriving to an extent that would have been seen as impossible a hundred years ago. The threats are still there: urbanisation, second homes, low wages in rural areas, crowded roads and the dominance of London as the centre of the world. Some of these problems existed a hundred years ago and were understood by Butterworth. He did not seek to stop the march of time but to preserve what was good and noble about England.

In this book I have tried to bring George Butterworth to life in a manner that is respectful. I have not engaged in unprofitable speculations. Some aspects of biographical writing involve probabilities; where an event cannot be proven to have taken place I have said so.

A seminal moment in the musical life of this nation that took place at the Three Choirs Festival in Gloucester Cathedral in 1910 was the first public performance of Ralph Vaughan Williams's *Fantasia on a Theme of Thomas Tallis*. We know that George was present and that Ivor Gurney, Herbert Howells and Vaughan Williams sat together during the second half of the concert after the performance of the *Fantasia*. Vaughan Williams wrote some notes on Howells's programme.

There is, however, no written record of George meeting Gurney and Howells in the cathedral. But it would have been most unusual for George not to have gone over to greet his friend Ralph after the concert to congratulate him on his outstanding composition. At this point Vaughan Williams would have introduced him to the two young men who were in a high state of excitement after hearing the *Fantasia* for the first time.

It is on record that both men paced the streets of Gloucester for hours and were so exhilarated by the music that they each spent a sleepless night.

The conversations between George and various people in this book are also based on probability and are there to illustrate and develop George's character. I make no apology for using my informed imagination in writing these conversations, considering them a necessary element in the accelerating tragedy of George's short life. A fundamentalist approach to biography can result in a very dull read; I make no excuses for putting words into George's mouth unless they are inaccurate or out of character. I rest my case with a quote from Michael Wright, co-writer with Stephen Grady of the excellent book *Gardens of Stone: My Boyhood in the French Resistance*: 'For the dialogue I have followed Thucydides' approach of attempting to convey if not what people actually said, then what they ought to have said at the time' (p. 419).

PART ONE

COMPOSER

Chapter One

Deerhurst

The pony and trap turned off the main road and headed towards the distant church tower rising from the trees. Warmth rose from the straight dusty road as the swaying conveyance drove north towards Deerhurst. Young George did not ask the obvious question; he knew that they would soon arrive at the church and meet his grandfather there. The journey from York had been long – hours on the train with multiple changes as they travelled south and west. The arrival at Tewkesbury via Malvern had been a surprise and the transfer to the trap sudden.

The trap contained young George, a silent observant eight-year-old, his father Alexander and an equally silent groom connected to the plodding Welsh cob by yards of supple leather reins. George was looking forward to seeing his grandfather at the church. He couldn't remember what he looked like but he could recall his voice. He knew that he was in a strange part of England called Gloucestershire where people sounded different and isolated hills dominated the flat landscape.

Few houses were visible as the road gently rose and fell. The church tower lay directly ahead; nothing spoiled the view. A low ridge to the east hid the wooded escarpment of the distant Cotswolds and the rounded hump of Bredon Hill to the north-east. As the trap surmounted the last hill before dropping down to the wide valley of the Severn, the Malvern Hills rose abruptly to the north. George knew instinctively that he was surrounded by different worlds – the hills and the presence of Wales to the west, the West Country to the south, the Midlands to the north and east. He liked maps and had studied a map of the west Midlands at his home in York before setting out on the long journey that was now almost at an end.

'Nearly there,' murmured his father. The trap swerved abruptly to the left away from the church tower to turn to the right past some cottages and a schoolroom, to come to a dusty halt just outside the iron church gate. There was total silence, only broken by the liquid call of a cuckoo far away beyond the sinuous flowing Severn.

Quick footsteps crunched along the gravel from the church. 'Welcome!' shouted George's grandfather, the Reverend George Butterworth. A tall, bald, grey-bearded man in knee breeches and a black stock strode up to the trap and lifted young George out and swung him on to the ground. He hugged him and then vigorously shook his son's hand. Turning to the groom he asked him to wait for a few minutes. The cob bent down to crop the grass while the groom stood looking at the distant hills. The reverend gentleman waved the weary travellers down the straight path towards the church. Although tired, father and son were happy to see the ancient church again. They were hungry and thirsty but that didn't matter; they were going to see something unique. The Reverend George pulled open the door of the church under its Norman arch. Just inside, in the dim and dusty interior, sat a tray of biscuits and a bottle of lemonade with two clean glasses.

'My housekeeper is on her annual holiday, so improvisation is the order of the day. We'll go back to the vicarage quite soon. No house can measure up to this house of God. I always feel that it is a privilege to be here, even after so many years,' said the Reverend George.

With their eyes making out benches and windows in the shadowed church, father and son drank gratefully and ate the crumbling biscuits. They stood below a Saxon tower with herringbone courses of stone and triangular windows high above them. Young George was absorbed by the ancient space enclosed by Saxon walls. He listened with rapt attention as his grandfather explained that his church had stood, with later additions, for eleven hundred years.

Alexander Butterworth found himself wondering about his son, his dark, intense son who, although often silent, never seemed bored. He was an observer, an adaptor, who always wanted to know where he was both geographically and in the scheme of things. Self-possessed and driven, he seemed much older than his eight years. His brown hair flopped unnoticed over his dark eyes.

Young George looked at his father. He loved him very much but felt that his father was different, serious, methodical and absorbed by business affairs. George knew that he could never be like his father. The distant cuckoo sounded again from beyond the river, unheard by Alexander. George was captivated by the haunting notes and their echoes reached him through warm summer air. He was no longer conscious of the ancient stones of the church all round him but transported high into the empty air above Deerhurst. He seemed to look down on the lonely church and its farms and cottages, with the sluggish Severn winding between its level banks.

The two men and George stood by the open door under the tower of the church. The westering sun had started to throw lengthy shadows of the trees along the church path. The interior of the church was growing dusky.

'Time to go,' said Grampa Butterworth. 'I've said evensong and it's time once more to lock up.' He produced an enormous key from his pocket and walked out into the dusk, followed by his son and grandson. There was a muffled metallic sound as the key turned in the lock and the three Butterworths walked towards the church gate in the luminous evening light.

'We shall have a proper look at the church tomorrow and at Odda's chapel nearby,' said Grampa Butterworth. Young George always thought of him in these terms. He had never known his grandmother. She had died many years earlier at the age of forty, leaving her husband alone and bereft to run the parish of Deerhurst. His grandmother had been the daughter of the Bishop of Lincoln and had been taken back to Lincolnshire for burial. Her husband had stayed in his parish and had learned to content himself with a life of solitude and devotion to God and to his parishioners. He was very near retirement and now considered his corner of north Gloucestershire to be home. Where he would go when he had to give up the living was something he hadn't yet seriously contemplated.

There had been considerable excitement in his life. A few years before, in 1885, the year of his grandson's birth, he had been sitting in the kitchen of an ancient half-timbered farmhouse on a slight mound only 200 yards towards the river from Deerhurst Church. The room was dim and had an earth floor. The Revd Butterworth had been sitting on an old settle with a cup of tea in his hand when he noticed that two of the windows behind dingy lace curtains were unusually long and had rounded windows. He stood up and asked permission of the farmer to look more closely.

The room he examined was at the north end of the farmhouse and was not made with a timber frame. The walls were plastered on the inside and cement rendered on the outside. Revd Butterworth felt a rising anticipation as he walked out of the narrow door into the small orchard surrounding the end of the building. He looked closely at the rendered wall and saw that in places the stonework showed through. Although there was no herringbone course the stones were laid in a way that could have been Saxon. Moving to the building's corner Butterworth made out long and short quoin stones beneath the rough render. With great eagerness he went back inside the dusty farmhouse room. More research would have to be undertaken but here, almost certainly, was a Saxon chapel that was not as old as Deerhurst Church. What a find! Praise be to God and to the man who founded the chapel sometime quite soon before the conquest of England by William the Bastard.

Young George Butterworth was feeling sleepy and contented as the swaying trap conveyed the three generations of Butterworths along the lane to the nearby vicarage, where a woman from the village would provide beds and supper. The song of the nightjar had replaced that of the cuckoo in the gathering dusk. Evening aromas rose round them: dew-dampened dust, honeysuckle, sheep. This must be the heart of England, thought George, as the soft rumble of his father and grandfather's voices barely reached him above the clatter of wheels on the gravel road. George's last thought before his head slumped on to his arm was, 'England'.

He woke up in bed a little while later, stretched and turned over, listening to the murmur of male voices from the next room.

'Yes, Father, he's very musical. He has a great appreciation of the beauties of God's world. I'm hoping that he will make a lawyer or a business-
man, God bless him. It's early days yet. We'll just have to see. ...'

George Sainton Kaye Butterworth, countryman and northerner, was
born on 12 July 1885 at 16 Westbourne Square, Paddington, West London.
His father, Alexander Butterworth, was a solicitor for the prestigious
Great Western Railway, at the time embroiled in the decision to abandon
Brunel's broad gauge and adopt the standard gauge used by nearly all other
British railway companies. His mother, Julia Marguerite Butterworth,
née Wigan, had been a professional singer before her marriage and
possessed a very fine coloratura soprano voice. She was musical and
artistic; her marriage with Alexander was a marriage of opposites but,
nevertheless, very successful. Her piano playing and singing enlivened
the house in Paddington and enchanted her baby son George, a serious
babe with brown hair and a very direct look. Alexander had an appreciation for music and also enjoyed his wife's playing and singing.

Six years after their son's birth, the Butterworths moved out of London
to the clearer skies of York, moving into 3 Driffield Terrace, The Mount.
They named their new house 'Riseholme' after the village north of Lincoln
where Alexander's mother was buried. It was a slightly Italianate early
Victorian house in a quiet street south of the city walls that ran parallel
to the main road that went south. A long garden lay behind the house
with an iron gate on to the Mount.

Alexander had accepted a job as a solicitor for the North Eastern
Railway, which had its offices just inside the walls of York. Before long he
had become General Manager of the railway company.

York suited George very well. As he grew into a small boy he appreciated
the ancient churches, mediaeval streets with their overhanging houses,
high defensive walls, and, above all, the music and bells of the Minster.

One evening Alexander set a challenge for his son. He had heard him
practising the piano and thought that he was rather good. But how
serious was he about the piano in particular and music in general? In the
comfortable chintzy living room he made a bet with his son: 'I'll give you
five shillings when you can play me the whole of "Rousseau's Dream". I

don't mind how long it takes you to master it. You seem to have it some of it off to a "t" already from what I have heard.'

'Tomorrow night, Papa. I'll play it for you in its entirety.'

The next evening after supper when the fires were lit and the heavy curtains drawn against the cold northern evening, father and son sat down in the drawing room. George adjusted the piano stool so that his feet could reach the pedals. He closed the music book and put it down on a table. Alexander sat in his armchair, his legs crossed. He did not feel as relaxed as he appeared to be and wondered if he had been too rash in setting the challenge. George had chosen the evening so his father must accept the gauntlet flung at his feet in his turn.

Confidently George began to play. His rendition of the whole piece was faultless and conveyed a feeling for the piece that was mature and measured. As the last notes died away Alexander knew that he needn't have worried.

'Bravo, bravo, my boy. Excellent! Here's your five shillings, which you fully deserve.'

George was obviously pleased but a puzzled look crossed his face. 'It seems a lot of money for so simple a task. But thank you with all my heart. I'll keep it for when I go away to boarding school.'

Alexander beamed at his son. Such an honest boy and no false modesty. No doubt he would go far in business or in his own chosen profession of law.

Soon enough it was time to go away to school. George was ten years old and it was felt that he should receive a more general education than the music provided by his mother and the education afforded by the local school. A future captain of industry should have a rounded education and the opportunity to mix with boys of his own class.

Chapter Two

Aysgarth

The future captain of industry arrived somewhat reluctantly at a slightly forbidding building considerably to the north of York. It lay in a valley between the rampart of the North York Moors and the softer Dales to the west. Aysgarth was a preparatory school for the sons of the upper classes who were expected to go on to Eton or other public schools and then hopefully to Oxford or Cambridge. It had only opened six years earlier.

George had his own ideas about his future. He would do nothing to upset his beloved mother and father but he would be his own man. After an initial impression that Aysgarth was austere and remote, George warmed to the place. He had his trunk sent up to his dormitory and was welcomed and shown round the school by the headmaster and his dog. George found that he liked the buildings and the rural setting and his headmaster, the Revd Thomas Hales.

Conveyed from the station at Thirsk by the school's carriage, George had made a note of the route south in case he should have to leave school in a hurry and make his way home. He kept the route at the back of his mind long after he had settled in to Aysgarth School.

A week or two into the autumn term George's music master, John Callow, and the head were talking in the latter's office.

'What do you make of young George Butterworth?' asked the head. There was a long pause.

'A singular boy. Most unusual. He's settled in well. He's a bit remote from the other boys. Very self contained, self-possessed really. He enjoys games but hasn't really applied himself to his academic work. He seems happy playing the piano and the organ. He's really good. Seems to be a Christian. He's even writing a hymn tune. I can't seem to pin him down, though. He looks one in the eye but gives nothing away. Doesn't seem to be afraid of anything, even a beating. He's happy enough but often seems to be somewhere else. A remarkable boy.'

The head answered: 'We must keep an eye on Master Butterworth. He isn't a conformist. That's no bad thing but it mustn't upset the other boys. He must have no special privileges. He will distinguish himself in some way. He could surprise us. We must keep him on our side.'

George, blissfully unaware that he was a subject for discussion, passed his days in classrooms, music studios, and on the football pitch. He slept well in the dormitory he shared with other boys and was bothered by no one. The only thing that affected him was the new boys who, like himself, had come from all over the country at the tender age of eight or ten years. Some of them were inconsolable; they were constantly in tears, missing their mothers, fathers, brothers and sisters. Gradually some of them subsided into lethargy, drifting through the long and varied days of school. Others never settled, became quiet and withdrawn, and faded into the daily routine. George wished that he could help these lost boys, save them from their quiet despair.

Perhaps he could do so through his love of music. He played the piano for hours when others went on healthy walks over the hills of north Yorkshire. While he also loved the hills, he preferred to walk alone, something impossible for a new boy of ten. Up his sleeve he kept his secret plans of escape if he should need them.

One cool day George was walking across the grass below the tower of the school. The air was crisp and there was a faint smell of autumn in the air; the tang of chestnuts and falling leaves. He noticed three boys standing under a group of trees beside the football pitch. There was something tense about the group. Two large boys of twelve or thirteen were leaning over a younger boy. Even from 100 yards away George could feel menace in the situation. He walked quickly over to the boys in time to catch the hissed words: 'Let's do the little bastard in.'

Walking straight up to the boys towering above him George said quietly: 'What's going on?'

'None of your business, new boy,' spat the largest of the boys.

The other boy swung his clenched fist straight into George's face. The pain was extreme but George managed to stay on his feet. He plunged his fist into the larger boy's belly, winding him. As he went down his friend took an indecisive step backwards. George, with tears of pain streaming down his face stepped towards him. The older youth turned and ran, his friend crawling away towards him. He dropped the coin that he had taken from the younger victim who stood, shaking, in front of George. George, bending painfully down, picked up the coin and pressed it into the small boy's hand.

'What's your name?' he asked.

'I don't want to tell you,' replied the boy in a shaken voice. 'But thank you for what you did.'

'I can't bear to see bullying,' replied George, blood now dripping from his nose. 'If those boys bother you again you must let me know.' Anger was beginning to replace any fear he had felt moments earlier. He wondered if the two youths would bother him and his new friend again. He would have to keep his eyes and ears open at all times and watch his back. He did not regret his hasty action; he would do it again. How dare two older boys menace a younger one who was in no position to defend himself?

George put his arm over the boy's shoulder and walked him back to the school buildings. He didn't care what happened in the future; what he had seen just wasn't right.

Next day, on the way out of the chapel, one of the boys who had been involved with the bullying incident took George aside.

'Fond of music are you, Butterworth?'

'Yes,' replied George.

'You mind your own business in future or I'll break some of your fingers for you.'

George looked up at the older boy whose hair fell untidily over his left eye. He said nothing but turned on his heel and walked away, expecting to feel a hard blow on his head or shoulders. Nothing happened as George walked away over the football pitch, but later the headmaster came up to George after evensong.

'Ah, Butterworth. You seem to be having some trouble with some of the older boys. Do you want me to have a quiet word with them?'

'No, thank you Sir. I will look after myself here, thank you.' George was relieved that the masters were aware of what went on at Aysgarth. But he determined never to run for help.

Life continued to settle down at Aysgarth. George enjoyed his daily plunges in the new swimming pool. He applied himself to Latin and Greek and even Mathematics. He found that he was good at most subjects. Science bored him but games were a constant delight. Nobody bothered him as he began to play the organ in the chapel, even participating in the occasional service on it. The Dales in all their changing seasons enfolded him. He adapted as the nights drew in and frost began to glaze the window panes. Walking in winter became a great joy; the bare trees stark against the sky marked the turning of the seasons. Clouds of rooks wheeled in the sky as autumn gave in to the iron grip of winter.

Just before Christmas, George was sent home to York for the holidays. He was delighted to learn that his slightly younger cousin Hugh was coming to stay for a few days after Christmas. He got on well with Hugh. The two boys were somewhat similar in character and interests, although George was dark and Hugh had curly fair hair. Both enjoyed playing games, particularly cricket. They would argue for hours about which was the best county team. Naturally George supported Yorkshire while Hugh, the 'southerner', followed the fortunes of Wiltshire, a minor county to George's way of thinking.

Christmas was a happy time in the Butterworth household. George was persuaded to play the hymn tune he had composed at school and Hugh came up by train from the south. There were the usual jokes about the 'frozen north' but Hugh was quite won over by his tour of York, finishing in the Minster under the vast vaulting lit by huge stained-glass windows. The two boys sat listening to the organist practise the voluntaries for the Christmas service. Hugh was enthralled but George seemed restless and strangely dissatisfied. He turned to his cousin.

'The problem with this music is that it is not entirely English, not really connected with here. It very fine in its way but brings to mind Germany or France rather than our own country. We need to look at England for our inspiration. We must be true to ourselves.'

'I see what you mean,' replied Hugh. 'But surely, music is music wherever it comes from.'

George gave him a dark look. 'And I suppose that cricket is cricket whether played by Yorkshire or Wiltshire.'

Hugh elbowed his cousin in the ribs. 'Unfortunately I must concede that you have a point. Of course Wiltshire plays much better cricket than Yorkshire.'

George smiled distantly. 'It is up to us to stick up for our country. It suits us better than any other. English music also suits us best, although we must appreciate the works of French and German composers. Their inspiration comes from where they live, from their history and landscapes. We must be happy with ours.'

Ignoring the angry glances of the Minster guides for disturbing the peace with their conversation, the two boys made their way out into the grey drizzle of a northern winter's day. Although it was only four o'clock in the afternoon darkness was oozing into the narrow cobbled streets and ginnels of York. The urgent bark of steam engine exhausts drifted over from the station just outside the city walls.

George and Hugh walked back to the house through streets thronging with Christmas shoppers. Their breath hung in cold clouds before them as they anticipated the warm fires and buttered toast waiting for them at home.

George played his hymn tune on the piano for the family on Christmas Day. He did not feel in the slightest part nervous of the performance but wondered if his composition would come up to the mark. It was warmly received but George's natural modesty made him want to forget the whole episode once it was over.

Soon it was time to go back to school. George felt ready to go. He wanted to be back in the countryside with its frosted grass, bare trees and water as hard as iron. There was an integrity about the bare bones of the winter landscape, an honesty that almost hurt. George wondered how he could share these strong feelings with others. One day he thought he might be able to do so through music.

The slow rhythm of the seasons continued, with the gradually lengthening days. Football was played in the spring term and George enjoyed his forays on to the cold pitch. From time to time he would look up at the tawny fells where weak sunlight gave promise of warmth to come. Rooks flapped in the tall bare trees, the twigs in their beaks foretelling the coming of new life.

George soon realised that he needed to concentrate on some of the subjects he was meant to be learning. English and Maths he found easy, but when it came to science he felt no affinity with the facts and experiments he was expected to perform. He did enough to get by but followed his enthusiasms where they would naturally take him. He surmised, correctly, that if he shone at games he would be forgiven for a less than wholehearted approach to the subjects he found less congenial.

With summer came cricket, which George adored. There was a natural rhythm to the game that he loved, a shifting emphasis on the roles of bowler, batsman and fielders that came together to form a whole greater than the sum of its parts. To George a game of cricket was rather like a symphony; the whole game was held together by the tension of the parts played by the various players. Sometimes the disharmony of a dropped catch jarred the rhythm of the game, sometimes the click of ball on bat was sweet and fitting.

Above all there was the chapel organ with its three consoles. George sometimes had the opportunity to play at evensong and other services. Many of his fellow pupils found George to be a preoccupied boy, not exactly unfriendly but often not engaging with them. He had a few really close friends with whom he could be frank and direct. With the other boys in the school he didn't feel that he could show this side of his character. So he stayed aloof and a little removed from most of his peers.

The years passed happily at Aysgarth. Well into his third year there the headmaster asked George to come to see him at the end of the school day. George knocked on his study door and went in on the command 'Come'. The head sat him down and noticed how the lad was growing up. As usual he needed a haircut and his eyebrows were darker than ever.

But he saw no trace of fear or submission in the boy, only mild curiosity.

'Well George, I won't beat about the bush. You have so far distinguished yourself here in music and in games. You have stood up for boys who were being bullied and have not been bullied yourself. You have made some good friends among the boys and the staff. Your qualities of leadership have enabled you to become school captain. However, you need to pull up your socks. You will be leaving us soon, hopefully for Eton. Entrance to this great school is by Foundation Scholarship examination. What could you be doing better to achieve your place at Eton?'

George smiled disarmingly at the head. 'Well sir, I think that I could concentrate much harder on my academic work. I should like very much to go to Eton where I will particularly enjoy the music, football and cricket. But, frankly, there is a tension in my life. I want to succeed in everything but I tend to concentrate on the things that give me the most pleasure.'

'Thank you, George, for your honesty. We are counting on your getting to Eton, however. We don't want you just to scrape in but to do yourself and the school proud. What do you say?'

'Put like that, sir, it is clear that I must indeed pull my socks up. I'll do you proud and to the best of my ability.'

George left the head's study determined to do just that. He spent much more time revising the subjects that did not come naturally to him. He kept music as a treat and a reward that had to be earned. Eye strain and headaches were to be his lot for the next few weeks. His friends left him alone and did not distract him. Many of them doubtless needed to attend to their own drooping socks.

Chapter Three

Eton

A few days after George had finished sitting his examination papers he was summoned once more to the head's office. Once more George knocked, feeling decidedly less confident than the previous time he had done so.

'Come!' thundered the head and George walked into the study. The head stood up behind his desk. 'George!' he bellowed. 'You've done it! Not only are you going to Eton but you came fourth in the entrance examinations. Well done sir!' George stood firm in front of the head, and shook his hand. 'Well, sit down man. I'd offer you a cigar if it were allowed. Never mind. You've done very well for yourself and for the school. We're all very proud of you.'

George sat down in front of the desk and thought of his parents. They would be delighted, of course. His cousin Hugh was a year behind him and was hoping to go to Marlborough. He looked forward to the summer holidays, to seeing his family and to a number of hard-fought cricket matches. Now, above all, he could go back to his music with a clear conscience.

His train journey back to York was bitter-sweet. He was sad to leave Aysgarth where he had been happy, sad to say goodbye to his close friends. The journey south through the Vale brought him home to York. He was delighted to see his parents again. They, in their turn, were overjoyed to see him and to congratulate him on his success.

The summer vacation settled down into music lessons, composition, cricket and warm days spent in a small pleasant city. George had a chance to think; he was about to cross a border. Eton was in the south, a different realm to George's adopted one. To him it represented a softer world, a less direct world, where an exaggerated form of dress distinguished the scholars of Eton College. There would be academic work, sport and music as well as the establishment of a natural order of precedence.

It was quite clear to George where the emphasis would lie. He would keep his own counsel. Music would always come first, then sport, then academic achievement. At some point he would have to reconcile his father to his choice. His mother would be no problem; music had always come first in her life. His father would want what he considered the best for his son; he appreciated his son's musical vocation but saw his future in the law or in industry.

The border would also be geographical and cultural. The south country was a distant memory. George understood the north, its directness suited him. He would be a quieter boy in the south, more watchful, more subtle and more guarded. In the meantime, he would enjoy York and work hard at his musical studies under his tutor.

Summer rushed on towards autumn. The pleasures of music and cricket accelerated what time remained to George in York. The century was also drawing to a close as Great Britain's queen, the aged Victoria, was approaching the end of her long life. Before the twentieth century arrived George would have settled into his new school, the venerable Eton College.

Soon enough it was time to go south. George's family said goodbye to him on the broad, curving platform of York Station. Warm sunlight flooded the busy station. Carriage doors slammed, shrill whistles blew and an engine blew off steam on a far platform. Alexander frowned at this extravagance then turned to his son standing by the door of the North Eastern Railway express.

'Goodbye my boy. Work hard and play hard in the soft south.'

George remembered that his father and his Uncle George had both been born and brought up in Deerhurst; not exactly the south but far from being the north. Deerhurst was yet another borderland, not quite West Country, not quite Midlands.

His father appeared to have read his mind. 'Eton is firmly in the south. Take from it all you can, but give to it all of which you are capable.'

George looked at his mother. She looked quiet, sad and a little frail. Saying goodbye was horrible even for a relatively few weeks. When he returned at Christmas so many things would have changed. He would have become an Etonian, used to wearing striped trousers and a top hat.

The guard blew his whistle and Alexander glanced at his pocket watch. Returning it to his waistcoat he murmured, 'On time as it should be.' With a quick peck on his mother's cheek George stepped aboard the train and sat down by the window in his first-class compartment. The train glided smoothly away. Looking out of the window through the haze of steam George saw his father take his mother's hand and pull her to him in an embrace. He suddenly felt very much alone.

The train surged south through the outer suburbs of York. George thought of his cousin Hugh, a year younger and still at prep school. He would have all this to go through in a year's time when he too would go as a boarder to public school.

Hugh lived in Swindon, like York very much a railway town. But he would go to Marlborough, only a dozen miles from his home. Here he would play cricket, rugby, football and hockey. His father, like his Uncle Alexander, was a solicitor. The two boys had much in common. It was a pity, thought George, that they did not live closer to each other.

The train raced on towards the south as the landscape flattened and became more arable. George felt vaguely depressed at the dullness of the countryside. After Peterborough he gave up looking out of the window and dozed with his head against the cool glass instead. When he woke up the train was diving into the first of the series of monotonous tunnels through the ridges of north London. Houses closed in on every side, streets of grimy yellow brick, plane trees, untidy cemeteries and dozens of omnibuses and Hansom cabs.

More sooty tunnels and the train slid, with a last despairing shriek, into the huge arched expanse of King's Cross Station. George stretched, rose to his feet, and opened the varnished door of his compartment. He climbed out and walked along the platform to the barrier where he showed his ticket and, stepping out into the forecourt, hailed a cab for the short ride to Paddington.

Entering Paddington he felt more cheerful. Here was somewhere that he remembered, somewhere familiar. The whistles, green locomotives and brown and cream carriages reminded him of a former existence that would become his life once again. The Great Western Railway, his father's former employer, was uncompromising, a force to be reckoned with. There was something strangely northern about it, something reliable and down to earth.

George's train left from Platform One. It dashed through the leafy London suburbs: Ealing, Southall, Hanwell, dull and solid, tree-lined and respectable. Iver Heath marked the end of London and the train soon slowed for Slough. George alighted and caught the branch line train for Eton. It rattled along the curved track and came to a halt in a small high terminus near the river. George made sure that he had enough change for a cab to the gates of Eton College.

For the next five years – fifteen long terms – George would live and work at Eton. He would go back north for the holidays and lead the dual life of an Etonian. As he slowly grew to manhood he became quieter, more shy in his everyday contacts, and more direct with his few close friends. He did not retreat into himself but devoted his time to music, athletics and games.

When George had been at Eton for a year, he learned that his cousin Hugh had been accepted at Marlborough School. He envied Hugh's nearness to home; Marlborough lay only a dozen miles from his home in Swindon. Like George, Hugh excelled at games, sometimes to the exclusion of his studies. Hugh was outgoing, generous and humorous – a capital chap.

George had soon forgotten about the escape routes to his home in York. He was getting too old for that sort of thing. His family would certainly not welcome him home from Eton during term time, so George committed himself to life in the south.

George's report at Christmas 1899, written by his housemaster Mr Lowry, hinted at a slight overconfidence: 'It is wholesome for him to learn this early that it doesn't pay to miscalculate the strength of a foe – I allude to the examiner rather than to Virgil.' It is clear that George was beginning to dig his heels in. Lowry wrote in April 1900: 'He is apt to be a wooden versifier. ... He says that unless he is in the top set [in Maths] he is doing no good.'

The new century arrived with fireworks and celebrations. Wise men looking over their shoulders at Great Britain's imperial past began to realise that it could not last forever. There were the beginnings of the stirrings of industrial unrest. The tacit acceptance of the ordinary people that they were inferior to those who controlled them was slipping. The roles of Church and State were slowly beginning to be questioned. Some men such as Alexander Butterworth moved with the times and were sensitive to the undercurrents of discontent. They valued the intelligence of humble men and women and respected them.

George himself was no snob. He often felt irked by the circles he moved in. Music was classless and should be for everyone. He felt that England was a wonderful country. Not perfect and not without its faults, but the beauty of the land, the towns and even the large cities was something to celebrate. The change was coming; much of it would be for the better but many wonderful things risked being swept away with the bad. With the advance of technology many old forms of music would pack up and leave. George was aware that pastoral England was changing as fast as the cities. Gramophones would replace much live music and many old songs, never written down, would either be preserved in one form or fade away into the amnesia of old people who sang as they went about their work or assembled in groups to sing and dance.

There was a certain frustration in being cooped up in Eton. There was Greek and Latin to be learned and many other subjects of greater or lesser interest to be studied. Sometimes academic work seemed an imposition when compared with music and games. George believed greatly in 'mens sana in corpore sano' – a healthy mind in a healthy body – and excelled in athletics and cricket.

When George had been at Eton some time he joined the Debating Society. He became quite well known for his blunt manner and forceful arguments. He also took part in the Eton Wall Game, where he showed a self-control and organisation of his teammates that many people noticed.

He was eventually elected to the Eton Society or 'Pops'. Twenty-five Eton boys elected him to the society when there was a vacancy. George's uncompromising manner might have been a problem to some of his masters, but seemed to have been appreciated by some of his fellow students at Eton.

From time to time the subject of young Butterworth came up among his masters.

'Butterworth seems to be more of a dry bob than a wet bob. He plays cricket superbly, has wonderful coordination and a good eye. He's not afraid of committing himself and being in the thick of it all. He's also an outstanding musician, plays the piano extraordinarily well, and composes beautifully. He's painstaking to the point of obsession and very critical of what he does.

I'm concerned that he is becoming rather withdrawn from some of the other boys. He doesn't suffer fools gladly and can be rather direct and blunt. He's very close with his friends and will always stand up for what he considers right. He has the rare quality of moral courage. He won't be bullied or moulded. He's a born leader when it comes to the things he considers of importance.

What I do sometimes worry about is his priorities. Will he commit himself to a career at the bar or as a solicitor? Does he, in fact, consider these things important? He's obsessed by music. Sooner or later he'll have to reconcile himself to the fact that he will have to make a living. He's very close to his mother and father but I see a clash coming. He's not rebellious but his quiet determination will upset his father if he eventually decides to make a career in music. I think he'd rather starve in a garret than become a lawyer.

He's definitely Oxford material if he puts his back into his studies. I think I must have a word with him in my study and suggest that he concentrate his mind on his academic work. Music, games and work must be balanced in a more realistic fashion in Butterworth's case. Which one of this trinity does he consider to be the most important?'

In George's mind the answer was obvious and always had been. Being in no part the politician he told his housemaster what he considered his priority to be.

'Sir, in answer to your question, it is music that will always come first, then games, then academic work. It would be dishonest to pretend otherwise. I see academic work as the means to an end rather than anything else.'

'I see, Butterworth, but how will you reconcile this view with your father's? He has high hopes for you in the legal profession or in one of the other professions.'

'I cannot pretend to be what I am not. I do not rule out a profession but music will always come first.'

'Well, Butterworth, you owe it to your family and to Eton to go up to Oxford and study for a degree. What you do with your life after that is, of course, your own affair. I wish you the very best of luck in your future and heartily suggest that you work much harder at your academic studies in order to achieve the best of which you are capable.'

'Thank you sir. I will pull up my proverbial socks. I won't let you down.'

During Butterworth's fourth term at Eton Queen Victoria, Great Britain's longest-reigning monarch, the 'dear old queen', finally died. With her died the nineteenth century, even though many of its virtues would continue. To emphasise the changing times her solemn funeral procession was filmed, a permanent flickering image of a draped gun carriage pulled slowly through the streets of London accompanied by soldiers in bearskins with rifles reversed.

George felt sad that the old queen had gone. He had heard of her all his life and even seen her occasionally in the distance on state occasions. He wondered what England would lose with her passing. She had been a remote figure, formerly tucked away on the Isle of Wight for many years. During the last few years she had come back somewhat into public life but now she was gone, an unknown but constant quantity.

But there were more immediate matters at hand. George occasionally played the piano in concerts at Eton. His performances were almost faultless yet he felt that they were not fully appreciated by the audience who clapped politely but without great enthusiasm. His academic work had improved as he applied himself more to it. His heart was not really in it, though, but he considered his housemaster's advice and treated French, Latin, Greek et al. as a means to an end. To him that end would always be composition and the performance of music.

At Eton George found much inspiration and help in the Precentor, or Director of Music, Charles Harford Lloyd, and particularly his assistant Thomas Dunhill. Both men steered him towards composition. Dunhill taught him the piano and encouraged him to write music. The result was a violin sonata, the 'Barcarolle', which finally roused the Eton audience to enthusiastic applause, a 'torrent' that continued after the performance.

'I think that we could call that a standing ovulation,' said one of George's few close friends.

'I suppose that it was not too awful but I'm determined to do better,' replied George, looking thoughtful. 'One can never rest on one's laurels, you know.'

So George grew into a young man of just above average height, with unruly brown hair and an athletic disposition. He still had much in common with his cousin: a dedication to playing games to win and wildly fluctuating academic grades. Hugh excelled in cricket, hockey and racquetball. George limited himself mainly to cricket.

There was a growing tension in George's life between what he wanted to do and what was expected of him. He carried his musical notebooks wherever he went and did enough Latin and Greek to get by. His masters and friends sometimes despaired of him. But there was something about George that one didn't challenge, an assurance that was unusual in a boy so young. There was an intensity about him, particularly in his eyes, that was fierce and private. He could be frank to the point of becoming outspoken. There was nothing false about him. One accepted him for what he was or one left him alone.

In George's Easter report in 1900, one of his masters, Mr R.P.L. Booker, wrote: 'A little more cordiality and geniality would win him more unstinted praise, but he does not appear to be of a demonstrative nature, and what is bred in the bone is difficult to alter.'

One summer George went up to Scotland, naturally by train. His father had advanced to become a director of the North Eastern Railway Company and carried, at all times on his watch chain, a silver medallion that enabled him to travel all over the nation on all the diverse railway companies that existed and competed at the time. He was a great believer in the positive role of the railways in trade and in taking people to see new parts of their own country.

The Butterworths arrived in smoky Edinburgh as the sun was setting over the Pentland Hills. They emerged from Waverley Station to look up at the castle on its crag and the steep roofs and chimneys of the Royal Mile rising to the heights. Trams swayed and clanged along Princes Street past the Scott Monument above its gardens. Then they turned back into the North British Hotel for a comfortable night with porridge and oatcakes for breakfast before setting out by train for the Highlands.

George's mother was becoming increasingly frail and was duly ensconced in the compartment, first class of course, and wrapped to the waist in a tartan rug. The window was closed tight against the smoke and reek of Edinburgh as the train set off for Perth and the tawny flanks of the Highlands beyond.

As his wife slept, Alexander leaned over and asked George what he would do in the Highlands. Would he go deerstalking, paint watercolours, or just walk the mountains?

George gripped his notebook. 'I shall enjoy the mountains and the lochs. I shall walk about and look and listen. But above all I'll compose music and note it all down in my book.'

'That's fine, of course,' replied his father, 'but don't neglect the rest of your life. Soon, I hope, you'll go up to Oxford and you must think carefully about how you are to make a living, how you are to devote yourself to advancing in the world.'

George looked pointedly at his father's watch chain and the medallion hanging on his waistcoat. 'Please be assured, dear Father, that I'll never let you down. But can you see me working in an office all day, week after week, year after year? I really don't have it in me. I cannot pretend that I can be what I am not. Please trust me Father.'

'God bless you my boy. I am what I am and you shall be what you shall be. Far be it that I should tell you what your future course of life will be. Just promise me that what you do will be the best of which you are capable.'

'Be assured that that will always be so.'

The summer was a great success. Some of the roses came back into George's mother's cheeks and Alexander walked and fished to his heart's content. After two weeks he went back to work in York but George and his mother stayed on at the lodge until early autumn and the shortening nights sent mother and son south again to York.

George, with full notebooks and a healthy outdoor tan, hoped that he could get a few games of cricket in before going up to Eton with its crumbling quadrangles and his equally crumbling academic record. All, however, was not lost.

The tension between what George wanted to do and what George was supposed to do came to the surface from time to time. Mr Booker kept up his conventional advice in George's reports in 1901 and 1902: 'The qualities of mind I want to see are a greater alertness and more suppleness. He will never make a first-rate scholar with such an air [of] abstraction and so rigid a manner' (August 1901). And 'There is waywardness about him which makes him jib at a distasteful or irksome task' (March 1901). There was also the comment: 'But I do wish he would drop his nonchalance' (April 1902).

Soon after George's report at Easter 1902, George's mother wrote, in quiet desperation, to Mr G. Brooksbank, George's former housemaster at Aysgarth. She asked Brooksbank to write to Eton about him. His reply was more enlightening than Booker's rants: 'I judge him to be an extremely sensitive boy – with the self-conscious artistic side of his nature highly developed – but he has reached an age when this might be explained to him … pity that George has not outgrown that rather unfortunate diffidence of manner that might so easily be mistaken by unsympathetic observers – it is a pity he cannot cultivate a more genial manner.'

But Booker was not the only master critical of George's 'nonchalance'. Mr C.H. Lloyd, of Savile House, George's music tutor, added his advice: 'Your boy is rather a problem. His aversion to technical work stands in the way of his real progress' (January 1903).

Mr Booker remained, however, George's bête noire: 'The chances of a scholarship to Trinity [College, Oxford] next Christmas are no doubt remote' (January 1903). He later remarked there was an 'unreadiness and forbiddingness of manner which at present tell against him' (February 1903). But Booker's praise of George's musical performance was much more positive: 'The orchestral piece done at the Concert seemed to a barbarian like myself a very remarkable performance' (April 1903). His parting shot, though, was completely in character: 'If he could take a more rosy view of himself and of the universe, it would impart a "sweetness and light" to his performance which would be worth a world to him' (March 1904).

No doubt George took a dim view of Booker's use of a cliché that so lacked originality of thought!

George narrowly failed the Newcastle scholarship exam because his Divinity and Latin verses were not quite 'up to scratch'. In the summer of 1904 George was accepted as a Commoner at Trinity College, Oxford. He was now an Oxford man apparently well on the way to becoming the lawyer that his father was hoping that he would become. So far so good, but a lot could happen in four years at Oxford.

His parents provided a gift of 'a very nice bowl' for Mr Booker 'which George thrust upon me last night' according to a thank-you letter to Sir Alexander and Lady Butterworth. There was no mutual love lost between George and Booker.

Chapter Four

Oxford

In October 1904 George set off once again for the south. His mother and father saw him off from York Station, waving bravely once more as the varnished teak carriages of the North Eastern Railway pulled away from the curving platform. As the distance increased George saw the diminishing figures of his parents obscured once more by drifting smoke. He settled down in his corner seat with his notebook and thought how fond he was of his parents.

As London approached, the countryside became flatter and more dismal. The hills of Hertfordshire raised his spirits and even the dark, sooty tunnels couldn't change his mood. The cab from King's Cross to Paddington rattled along past shops and parks. There was something about London, George had to admit, that was familiar and somehow cosy, even in its sprawl and vastness.

The train from Paddington to Oxford lifted his spirits further. The vale between the Chilterns and the Cotswolds far to the west was green and pleasant. The River Thames made its unhurried, circuitous way towards London through small stone and brick villages, past flint churches and woods. Here was approaching the heart of England, unchanging and far from the industrial Midlands and North.

The view of Oxford from afar was stirring. Domes, spires and towers rose above the chimneys and rooftops. Woodland seemed to enclose the town from encircling hills. This, George decided, would be a place of discovery and growth, a place of new friends and occasional inspiration. He liked what he saw and was open to Oxford's possibilities.

George also liked what he saw of Trinity College. It was smack in the middle of Oxford, opening on to Broad Street in one direction and Museum Road in the other. It was next door to Blackwell's Bookshop and was a spacious green island with extensive lawns and gardens, trees and court-yards. Behind the tall college gates the rumble and clatter of traffic seemed far away.

But so did the real world of rural villages, alehouses and village greens where old men danced and made music. At least Oxford did not lie far from the countryside and had a certain charm of its own. George was beginning to understand that, in Oxford, things were done differently to the rest of the world, academic and otherwise.

Soon after settling in at Trinity, in October 1904 George wrote home: 'I am in excellent health now, and getting through a certain amount of work. I hope shortly to increase the average per diem, but constantly going out to breakfast and tea is a distinct handicap at first, and one cannot afford to refuse invitations just yet.' He thanked his parents for sending various articles that he had forgotten and teased them for not having sent him a rope ladder.

Quite soon after arriving in Oxford George met a very athletic young man. Noel Chavasse was one of the twin sons of the Bishop of Liverpool. He entered Trinity College at the same time as George and was studying medicine. The two men got on well but their very different timetables meant that their paths hardly ever crossed after their initial meeting. George soon realised that Noel had a practical side that he lacked, an intense interest in technical matters and an analytical approach to how things worked. This made George feel sometimes at a loss when he compared himself to Noel.

Once settled into his rooms George wore his black gown, attended lectures, studied from time to time and established a music circle. One day he was introduced to an older man who would become one of his closest friends and musical confidants.

Ralph Vaughan Williams was tall, intense and slightly untidy. His shaggy hair lay over a strong brow. His eyes held a directness that George could identify with. He wore a rough tweed suit with matching waistcoat; George had to keep reminding himself that Vaughan Williams was a composer rather than a farmer or a country doctor.

'You must call me Raif, never Ralph. The old form is traditional and that appeals to me. I live in London and compose from time to time. I'm also engaged in collecting old folk songs and country tunes before they disappear entirely from England.'

'Yes, Raif, England is an inspiration. Change is in the air and much could be lost in the next few years. Gramophones and phonographs could replace the old ways of making music. I applaud what you are doing and should like to know more about it. I feel that, in the composition of music, England should be our inspiration. We have relied too heavily on the German and, to a lesser extent, French composers. Now it is our turn and we must grasp it. I do not denigrate foreign composers but it is our turn at last. Music flows from the people and you are doing valuable work in recording it.'

Vaughan Williams warmed to the younger man. He had heard that George could be taciturn and that he did not suffer fools gladly. Not that he considered himself a fool in any way. He was happily married and thirteen years older than George. His musical career had not developed as quickly or as steadily as he would have wished and although he had composed a few good pieces, time was marching on and he was now in his thirties. In George he saw his younger self with opportunities in the future that he himself might not have. But jealousy was not part of his nature and he certainly wished George well.

'When you finish at Oxford you should enrol at the Royal College of Music. You're reading Greats here but I feel that is not where your future lies. You will achieve good grades but you will have to choose what is most important to you. At the moment I work as an organist and choir-master at a London church. Composition is my passion but one also has to make a living. The rent and the bills must be paid if one is not to starve in a garret, so to speak.'

Life continued in a pleasant fashion for George at Oxford. He grew a lux-uriant moustache of which he was rather proud and enjoyed smoking a pipe. He worked somewhat harder at his composition and his music than his Greek, Latin and Ancient History. When it came time to take his Part One examinations he put on a spurt and gained a Second. This, he felt, at least gave him a breathing space.

More to his liking was his growing friendship with Ralph Vaughan Williams, which included visits to his London home, meeting his wife, and planning trips into East Anglia and Sussex to collect folk songs. An interesting future beckoned, the only cloud on the horizon being an eventual choice of how to earn a living. But, meanwhile, there were games of cricket to play, music to rehearse, discussions to be entered into and the odd book to read and study from time to time.

Then came the bombshell. In the early summer of 1906 George learned from his father that his cousin Hugh was leaving University College, Oxford, without taking his finals in order to go to live in New Zealand with his father.

'Why are they going so soon and so suddenly?' George asked his father.

'Like myself my brother is a solicitor. He and his partners in Swindon have encountered a bit of a problem. Not only did he invest nearly all his money in a "safe" speculation but he also risked a considerable amount of his clients' capital in the scheme. It seems that most solicitors do this kind of thing. It's not so much dishonest as short-sighted and over-confident. The upshot of this speculation is that he was hoodwinked and is now almost penniless. He has paid off his clients but the firm will be broken up and he will go back to the wool trade. And the best place for that is New Zealand.

He always was a bit of a dreamer, a tremendous enthusiast who could be quite carried away by tennis, cricket, or a misguided investment. I shall miss him very much when he is on the far side of the world.

Hugh has decided to join him and to support and help him. He is similar in many ways to my brother. It is possible that his finals at Oxford could have turned out to be as disastrous as his father's investment. We'll never know. He distinguished himself in sport at Oxford. His performance in hockey, cricket and athletics were notable, although his ankle injuries prevented him from gaining a blue in either hockey or cricket.

Both he and his father should do well in New Zealand. They get on well with people and follow their instincts. My brother's wife, your aunt, will follow him out there when he is settled as a wool broker. His daughters are generally settled here in England so I expect that most of them will stay here. It'll be a great wrench for them in any case.'

George left his father very quietly. He had a lot of news to absorb and much thinking to do. Hugh very much resembled George's father. He was loyal and enthusiastic, and far more outgoing than George. In his sudden departure George could see a spectre of his own future – great enthusiasm in one direction, a lukewarm interest in others. If he were to be truthful he envied Hugh's departure from Oxford just before finals. He couldn't see himself setting up as a country solicitor behind a polished brass plate earnestly talking to clients and poring over endless law books. There was music and cricket, and nothing else really seemed to matter in comparison.

He still had two years at Oxford to acquit himself well. He went back to his scores, his notations, his piano and organ, and occasionally his Greek and his Latin. He loved the city of Oxford, the river and the country-side. If he stood facing west he could imagine the endless villages, fields and woods and hills that led to Deerhurst, where his grandfather had rested in the churchyard for over ten years. His Uncle George and Hugh would miss Deerhurst very much; it had always been one of their favourite places.

Only music could distil the essence of such a place, bring back the sighing of the wind surging over the hills to rattle the reeds beside the Severn. Only music could take one back there from halfway across the world. This is what life should be about. How many people really knew that? With whom could one talk about such things at Oxford? Only a few men understood such things. Ralph was one man who understood that music was life itself.

During the vacations George set out to collect the music made by the people of rural England. He knew that it was fast disappearing and had to be written down and even recorded.

On a hot and dusty day Ralph and George set out on bicycles for Sussex. They left London by train with their mounts stowed safely in the luggage van. At Ardingly they retrieved their heavy bicycles, tipped the porter who had wheeled them carefully out of the van and set off down a long lane over a stony surface. Ralph wore his high-waisted tweed trousers and waistcoat. He pedalled along, occasionally pausing to brush his untidy fringe from his eyes. George followed close behind, smelling the rank hogweed in the hedges and the good country smells of grass and manure. They flew under tall elms, beeches and oaks, bright sunlight alternating with dappled shade.

Soon they came to a village green with a leisurely game of cricket being played by men of different ages and skills. The two men stopped for a minute to watch and to get back their breath.

'What I like about this game is the complete lack of self-consciousness of the players,' said George. 'They all try their hardest to score runs, bowl and catch out the members of the other team, but they're just in it for the fun of the thing.'

'That's quite right,' replied Ralph, his broad face shining with sweat. 'And that's how it is when one of the old men or women sings an ancient song from the country. He might be slightly drunk, flat or sharp, have no teeth and a face as wrinkled as an old apple. But the performance will be good because it is real and well remembered. The song could go back hundreds of years and be recalled by only a few. This is why we have come here, to capture and record the old songs before they are forgotten. Most people couldn't care less if these beauties are lost. They will have their phonographs and gramophones and never themselves sing from one day to the next. These old songs remind them of the hard times and of unspeakable labour. But what will the future bring to this land of ours?'

'We won't hear any music but the sound of leather on willow if we stand here,' said George. 'Let's go into the public house over there and seek out beer and music.'

The two men leaned their mounts against an oak and walked into a low building advertising itself as 'The Three Tuns'. Sitting on a settle in the corner near the grate of the fireplace Ralph raised his voice to the few old men who sat companionably at the bar.

'Gentlemen, would any of you sing us a song in here? Not a recent music hall song but an old country song. I'll buy anyone who will sing

to me and allow me to write it down a pint of best bitter.'

'Well zur, I reckon uz can do that for 'ee. I haven't zung for many a long year but, if you can stand it, yer goes. ...'

The old man stood by the bar and cleared his throat. He looked hard at the pewter tankard in his hand and put it down on the bar. Ralph nodded to the landlord who filled the tankard with ale from a tilted barrel behind the bar. Then the man began to sing. His voice rose and cracked, swooped and droned but soon got into the rhythm of the song. The words were hard to make out but had something to do with apples and honeysuckle. There was an incredible sweetness in the song which transcended the occasional stumbles and false notes. The man was small and bent, a figure in ragged trousers with yorks below the knee and a filthy collarless shirt that had once been white. His song took on a life of its own, a rhythm and cadence that was beautiful.

He finished suddenly, with his head cast down with a sudden self-consciousness. George and Ralph were in raptures. The old man smiled and took a long pull from his tankard.

'Excellent!' shouted Ralph. 'Please, sir, would you sing it for us just once more?'

The countryman sang again, this time with far more confidence, while Ralph scribbled down the words and George noted the score. Another pint was offered and accepted while the old man's friends clapped him on the back and shook his hand.

'Us hadn't heard the likes of that for many a long year.'

'Didn't know you had it in you Sam.'

'Noisy ole bugger i'n you!'

George and Ralph left the pub happy men. They had the feeling that they had awakened memories long dormant. One more old song had been saved from oblivion.

Soon afterwards George heard of a group in Oxfordshire who sometimes performed an ancient dance. It all sounded rather vague but research in the college library uncovered an antique form of dance once favoured and encouraged by King Henry VII known as 'morris dancing'. The word 'morris' was an apparent corruption of 'Moorish'.

It all seemed rather exciting so George put aside an essay on Herodotus and set off on his heavy bicycle for a distant village. He envied Edward Elgar his enthusiasm for his mount, which he referred to as 'Mr Phoebus'. However, he was young and fit and anything would be better than wrestling with Herodotus. Fortunately most of Oxfordshire was fairly flat, unlike Elgar's Malvern Hills.

When George reached the distant village, which nestled almost against the Cotswolds, he parked his bicycle and strolled over to the inn, a low stone building with a roof composed of graded slabs of grey stone. He heard the plaintive sound of an accordion coming from behind the building and followed its strains through the bar to a stable yard behind.

There were six strangely dressed grey-haired men and an even older man sitting on a backless chair with an ancient squeezebox in his hands. Such was the concentration that nobody saw George leaning in the inn doorway for several minutes.

The six dancers swinging around and leaping up with a vitality that belied their years made George think of the green man carved into the stonework of many an ancient church. They were so wonderfully pagan with their faded ribbons, grubby white shirts and sashes crossed at the chest. A couple wore masks that seemed to resemble the heads of stags. They had no notes or instructions to remind them what to do but danced on in almost perfect order. Their hobnailed work boots scraped the cobbles of the yard as they twirled and turned.

The music came to a strange and triumphant crescendo and then ended. The dancers relaxed and finally noticed the young man with the brown moustache, untidy hair and notebook. Hands were shaken and George had many questions to ask and answers to note down in his book. He made a record of ancient tunes and their variations, where they came from and how long they had been played. He copied down the dance steps and asked to be taught how to perform them. His efforts were well received, even if his infrequent mistakes were the cause of much healthy laughter.

George ordered beer for all the men and sat down with them in the low, dark bar. The murmuring sound of voices continued for a long time. George learned that morris dancing sides had been far more numerous and competitive years before. One old man told him, with relish, that he had very much enjoyed the fighting between competing morris sides when he was a young man. When George looked up he realised that he must go back to Oxford and to Herodotus. He bade the dancers farewell, with many a sincere thanks and a couple of silver shillings to the bagman. This was reality, a living dance that went back hundreds of years, still performed for the sheer pleasure and enjoyment of disciplined movement accompanied by haunting tunes.

This was truly the music of the people, a vital performance connected with the times of the farming year. It was pagan and linked George to his distant forebears in the north and in the west. There were memories of historic events in these dances, of life and loss, of death and rebirth. This was truly wonderful and yet was dying out rapidly all over the country.

George's friends Ralph, and an older man by the name of Cecil Sharp, were doing wonderful work in writing down the tunes and recording where they had come from. In the changing world every village would one day look like every other village as farming became more standardised and began to employ less men on the land. Already, steam traction engines and machines were replacing men on the land. For years farming had been in recession and the price of land was falling. Towns were growing outwards like bramble thickets; brick houses were covering the green fields and stretching along the roads from one town towards another.

It seemed to George that Oxfordshire with its broad vale rising to chalk and limestone hills was close to the centre of England. It was still far removed from London and sat below the Midlands between the slanting Chilterns and the distant Cotswolds. As he rode slowly back to Oxford he thought about how important the old customs and ways of England were. They must be collected so that they did not die. They must not be pickled like calves' feet but performed, developed into new themes while the old tunes were kept safe for ever. Because nothing ever stood still; something as dynamic as a 'folk' tune was constantly evolving and changing as it went from place to place, from performer to performer.

The problem to George was how to make a living from these old forms. How to adapt them to new and vital forms? Composers and musicians no longer commanded patrons. Compared to a barrister or solicitor a composer made very little money. And so back to Herodotus. He was fine in his way but his words did not stir the soul in the same manner as an ancient song born of the English countryside and sung by a wrinkled, toothless man in a quavering high-pitched voice that raised the hairs on the back of one's neck.

George's final year at Oxford passed in a heady mixture of collection, adaption, composition and performance. A few good friends made his life bearable and encouraged him in his music. Dr Hugh Allen, a gruff but amiable man, became his mentor and lifelong friend. Ralph Vaughan Williams was also a close friend, and Cecil Sharp, another great collector of folk songs, completed the circle. All three men were older than George but considered him an equal as a composer and performer of music.

Before taking his finals George had one important matter to sort out. During the Easter vacation he travelled up to York to see his parents. He walked from York Station to Driffield Terrace, having ordered his luggage to be delivered by cart.

Sitting in the tree-shaded garden, with the occasional sound of passing traffic hushed by the vigorous sound of birdsong, he leaned forward towards his father.

'Father, I've decided that I cannot study for the bar nor can I become a solicitor. I just don't have it in me. Believe me Father, I've thought about it long and hard. I've even prayed about it. My mind is made up and there's no going back. I'm determined to pursue a musical career. I shall continue to compose, arrange and perform music. No doubt I'll have to find work to support myself while I do this. I'm determined that this is what life holds for me and that nothing else will do for me.'

Alexander sat very still and said nothing. His face went very red and then pale. He looked sadly up at his son.

'Very well George. I'll not pretend that I feel a keen disappointment. I will not force you to do what you will not do and I will not prevent you from following a musical vocation. You would make a very fine lawyer. Your life now will be a struggle until you become well known and perhaps even after that. Your mother and I know what a fine composer you are. But how many composers earn a living wage from their work? I can think of very few and most of them are from wealthy families with private incomes.

What I will do is this. I shall settle on you a small annual income so that, at least, you shall not starve. It will not be enough to live off and so you will strive to earn your own money. In this way you have my blessing and love. I know that you will succeed but the road ahead is hard and stony.

I am no longer angry but resigned. Far be it for me to tell you what to do or how to lead your life. We will enjoy our time here together in York and then you must devote yourself to your studies in preparation for your finals. We want you to do well as a scholar as well as a musician. You are an Oxford man and will be remembered as such. God bless you.'

For once George was lost for words. He had expected either a storm of angry words or sullen acceptance. His father must have been thinking this matter over for a very long time. He had spoken with a wisdom that George hoped he would one day acquire.

The vacation passed quickly, with the anticipation of sitting his finals like a lead weight in George's stomach. In a way he envied his cousin Hugh, now happily teaching at a boy's boarding school at Wanganui half-way across the world on the North Island of New Zealand. Hugh played cricket 'down under' all through the English winter, writing wittily and regularly to George and his family. George envied Hugh his outgoing nature and his acceptance of changing circumstances. Hugh's father, ever the optimist, was doing well in the wool trade and was happy to leave his past misfortunes behind. George admired a man who refused to be defined by a drastic change in circumstances.

After Easter, George left the family home for the last time. He knew that he would be back, but that he would be a visitor, a man making his way in the world with a little help from his father. Life was not going to be easy, but with hard work and determination he would make his way in the demanding world of music.

Soon enough the finals were upon him. The dreaded morning came grey with drizzle when the result of his hard work, or lack of it, would be assessed. He walked to the examination hall determined to do his best but with the sure knowledge that his eventual result would not be as good as he would have wanted it to be.

Each exam brought its own catharsis. Periods of frantic scribbling alternated with times of blankness, fatigue and frustration. Eventually it was over and George felt wrung out and hollow. A few days' rest and some walks beside the river would clear his brain before he could take his leave of Oxford. He would keep in touch with his group of friends, most of whom shared his passion for music.

A few weeks after his final examinations George learned how he had done. He had achieved a third-class degree. This result wasn't a disaster but it also lacked the distinction of a higher grade. It would do; considering the time that George had spent on his music during the last three years it was a reasonable result.

Chapter five

The Times, Radley College and The Royal College of Music

George settled down to find a job that would be congenial to him and would hopefully have some connection with music. He wrote letters, attended interviews and soon secured a job that he felt would suit him, at least for the foreseeable future.

In the summer of 1908 George moved down to London where he lived at 10 Torrington Square, close to London University. He went to work as an assistant music critic on *The Times*. He worked with H.C. Colles under the chief critic J.A. Fuller-Maitland. He did not enjoy what he did but he gained a reputation as a frank and outspoken critic. He wrote well and cut through what he considered to be 'humbug'. With a growing reputation for honesty and moral courage he soon became known for his mature breadth of musical judgement.

After working for nearly a year at *The Times* George decided to leave. He was sick and tired of being a commentator, a spectator. He had learned a lot about other men's work and other men's compositions and performances, but it was time for him to take a more active role. He was well thought of and for this he was grateful, but for him it wasn't enough.

In 1909 George moved west along the River Thames to St Peter's College, Radley, a public school in Oxfordshire. He was glad to be out of London and back in the countryside of England. He took a leaf out of his cousin Hugh's book and decided to become a teacher. In this way his life would be active with increased opportunities for composition and performance.

He would play cricket and football and walk in the country. Teaching would not be easy and would sometimes try his patience and exhaust his finite reservoir of tolerance. But it would be good for him and he would make the best of it. He would also not have far to go in his free time to continue to collect folk songs and morris dances in Oxfordshire and the Cotswolds. Much would be available to him by train and bicycle.

George had kept contact with his good friends in Oxford and London, often visiting Ralph who had lived not far from him in the capital. He had continued his visits to the remoter parts of England with him and had also begun to collect and arrange folk songs with Cecil Sharp. As an early member of the Folk Song Society, George met many similar-minded people. He also began reading the poems of A.E. Housman, which had a lingering melancholy that appealed to him. Many of Housman's poems made him think of Deerhurst, his grandfather's old parish, a place that had woken him to the beauty of the English landscape and its essential simplicity. Housman was often morbid and fatalistic, but captured the spirit of a land that was changing with a remarkable stoicism. His poems were deceptively simple but beautifully crafted. To George he made the difficult art of poetic composition look easy.

Arriving at Radley by train, George liked the look of the school. It reminded him vaguely of Aysgarth. He wondered if he were outgoing enough to teach boys of differing abilities and with varying interests in music. He was determined to make his musical mark on a school where he soon found out that neglect of music had been rife.

Radley was a public school founded in early Victorian times with a marked Anglican emphasis. The boys who were pupils there were the leaders of the next generation of Englishmen and expected to act as such. They played games to win but music was not high on their agenda. Nevertheless George took charge of teaching the piano and of reviving the Choral Society, which had declined into oblivion a few years earlier. He took part in occasional concerts and recitals.

Given the Lodge House to live in, he found it was spacious and self-contained with an iron railing separating it from the road and the drive and a cherry tree on the lawn behind the house. This young tree reminded George of Housman's poem 'Loveliest of Trees' about the passing of time.

The drive beside the lodge led gently uphill, soon becoming an avenue of young chestnut trees. The cricket pitch with its quaint pavilion was sited on a plateau at the top of the hill beyond the school buildings. The music department was located just downhill from the cricket pitch. The brisk walk up the avenue to the classrooms and practice rooms gave George time to clear his head before the day's often exasperating teaching of groups and individuals.

He became known as an enthusiastic player of cricket, racquets and fives. In this way the frustrations of imposing music on a largely philistine group of boys was dissipated on the games field and in the fives court. His dream of training an instrumental band was never to be realised. George felt that he could keep his frankness in check no longer and decided to leave Radley after two terms of teaching there. He considered that the school was no place in which to improve his techniques and was too stifled there to compose a great deal. He was remembered fondly as a man whose strength of character forced him to move on – a 'man too big to be enclosed' by religiosity and limited horizons. He felt badly that he had failed to establish an orchestra at the school.

George's next move was one he had been somewhat dreading. He was now twenty-five years old and beginning to compose music for some of Housman's poems. His next logical step was to finish his formal musical education by going to the Royal College of Music in London. By good fortune, Alexander Butterworth and George's mother moved from York to London in 1910 and were able to offer George a home at their house at 19 Cheyne Gardens in Chelsea. There were advantages for George: Cheyne Gardens was quite close to Ralph's house, as well as being at no great distance from the Royal College of Music.

The day was bright, the birds sang, the liquid call of the cuckoo rose from a distant tree. The haunting notes, now far, now near, drifted over warm fields and dusty hedges to the group of dancers on the village green. The six men leaped and turned to the lively accompaniment of an ancient accordion. Handkerchiefs fluttered in their hands and were jerked in the same direction and then back again.

'This is capital,' exclaimed George to Cecil Sharp. 'I think I'm picking it up. It doesn't seem too hard to me, although it has its challenges.'

'Let's give it a try,' Cecil replied. 'In a minute it will be our turn. They won't mind at all; it will give them something to laugh at.'

When the dance ended the red-faced dancers lay down in the grass and rested. George and Cecil stood up and took off their jackets. They loosened their ties and pressed a coin into the bagman's hand. A few murmured words and the accordion player was ready.

The two men danced carefully, looking from time to time at the ground, at each other and at the accordionist. They lifted their heads as they gained in confidence. George seemed particularly at home after a while and, although sweating profusely in the hot afternoon sun, jumped and crossed his legs, swung his arms and shook his rather grubby handkerchiefs. With a triumphant note the music ended and the two men bowed from the waist as the six men clapped enthusiastically.

'That's proper,' cried one of the old men. 'You'm learning the Cotswold morris. You are the boys to carry it on when we'm too old and stiff to dance.'

Despite the heat of the day, all eight of the men continued to dance together, George and Cecil learning new steps and practising the ones they had recently learned. To George the steps and the music melded together so perfectly that dancing became akin to playing an instrument.

In the pub late in the evening when the dancers had gone home to their cottages in the village, Cecil leaned conspiratorially over the table and said to George: 'There are two ladies that I'd very much like you to meet. Their names are Maud and Helen and they are very keen on dancing, especially the morris and folk dancing. Maud is slightly older than you. She is helping me with the collection of songs and dances and works as my part-time secretary. Helen is younger and both are using dancing in the east end of London to help some of the young people there. They're very much in tune with the people there, being originally from Germany. They are Jewish but not of the faith. I'm very fond of both of them and of the good work that they are doing.'

After a few pints of beer some of George's natural reticence was receding. 'I'd very much like to meet them both and dance with them. I'm sure that women used to dance in morris teams.'

'Indeed they did, but not always in gym tunics,' replied Cecil.

'You make them sound all the more attractive,' said George.

'Truly they are. And they have sound heads on their shoulders. Maud is drawn to the suffragette movement. Both have socialist leanings, which I somewhat share. I somehow think that you do too.'

George's curiosity was piqued. He would have been the first to admit that his world was predominantly male. He lacked the small talk required to talk to ladies and was shy, often reduced to silence by the sight of a beautiful woman. He felt that he didn't know many women. After all, they didn't play cricket and were often absorbed in their own affairs. The Karpeles sisters seemed to have a lot in common with him.

'A penny for your thoughts,' Cecil broke in on his reverie. 'How are things going at the Royal College of Music?'

'Not too well, I fear. I've met some top notch people and have improved my playing technique on piano and organ but feel somewhat stifled from the creative point of view. This is where I should be, out in the fields and woods of England collecting, interviewing, filling my book with notes and, above all, composing. I just can't do that in a dusty room in London.'

'You remind me of Edward Elgar and his trusty bicycle Mr Phoebus, riding all over the Malverns and right over to the Welsh border. That's how it's done!'

'It seems to me, Cecil, that the clouds of war are gathering on the eastern horizon. What is the kaiser playing at? It's no good thinking that we're safe because he's a cousin of the king. The tsar of all the Russias is also a cousin and he seems to be as mad as a kipper as well. I think that we are increasingly under threat from Germany. I'm very sorry about that because I am very fond of the country, the people and the music. I feel we have a lot in common with the Germans but I don't trust the kaiser and his ambitions.'

'What will you do, George, if it comes to war? Will you go and fight the nation that produced Beethoven, Brahms and Schubert?'

'I really haven't thought about it very much. I shall have to play my part like every Englishman, I suppose. But I don't like the idea of killing men who speak German instead of English at all. Perhaps it won't come to war. I do hope it won't.'

'Housman saw it coming at the time of the South African War. He saw "the Lads in their Hundreds" go off to war and many never came home. His whole tone is one of melancholy and loss. If war is coming it will be infinitely worse than the war against the Boers. I fear that it will be "the Lads in their Thousands".'

'Yes, Cecil, Housman certainly has a point. He is very keen on his lads as well as on his country. There are other threats to the England we love: industrial unrest, rural depopulation, increasing mechanisation. We must hurry up and record the songs that are fast disappearing from our land. Soon they will be gone with the wine, so to speak.'

The two men fell silent. George returned to wondering about the very attractive Karpeles sisters.

Life at the Royal College of Music was becoming increasingly tedious to a man who knew what he wanted and what he wished to do. Composition was George's raison d'être; it was the end rather than the means that was important. Impatient with classes on French and German composers, he perfected his playing of the piano and the organ but longed to spend his time on composing music. His inspiration had become rooted in the English landscape, the fragile old England that was menaced and threatened on every side. There was a beauty in the unselfconscious simplicity in lives that were changing as poverty or increasing wealth altered how they lived and saw their worlds. Elements of rural England must be preserved and made public. Perhaps people would then understand what made England great. It was not its waning empire or declining power but the simple values of the English shires and the straightforward lives of the ordinary folk who farmed it, shaped it and enjoyed it.

George was happy that he was not alone in his view of England. Edward Thomas, a remote, high-shouldered writer, would leave his devoted wife Helen and his young family to walk the length and breadth of rural England recording his observations and thoughts in print. He was sometimes briefly accompanied by a mysterious stranger who, at the same time, attracted and repelled him. This man was another facet of Thomas himself, who was often torn by guilt. He found his young family irksome and boring while loving them to distraction. He needed time away from them to appreciate them, a fact that his wife fully and strangely understood.

George had no such ties or attachments. Love and marriage might come to him one day but must of necessity come unbidden. He wondered how Ralph could combine composition and domesticity. In a way he envied the fact that he could. Ralph had the easy social manner that George lacked. This brought George back to how he would get on with Maud and Helen Karpeles.

He would find out before very long. London was stifling him and he needed to get out into rural Oxfordshire to walk and dance. He boarded the train to Kemble with Cecil and joined the Cotswold morris team. Among them was a young man named Douglas Kennedy, very sure of himself and outspoken, and, at last, the Karpeles sisters.

Both women were in their middle twenties, dark, determined and, in their way, beautiful. Maud was the elder, the dominant sister. Helen was quieter and, to George, sweeter. They had lovely dark hair and handsome faces. They were serious but also laughed a lot. A glance of their brown eyes would put George in his place. He was here to dance, to study the steps and the music and to perfect the morris. It was fun but it was also a solemn business that must be performed well or not at all.

There was a great thrill in dancing well. It made the blood sing in pure pleasure as if nothing in the world mattered as much. The thump of feet on the grass, the plaintive sound of the accordion, the rhythm of the dance; it was all pure pleasure. The look on Maud and Helen's faces during and after a good dance made it all thrillingly worthwhile.

Life was certainly more pleasant away from London. In the summer of 1910 George went to Gloucester where a piece of Ralph's music was to be performed for the first time in the cathedral as part of the Three Choirs Festival. It was greatly to George's satisfaction that the piece was called *Fantasia on a Theme of Thomas Tallis*. This would be a truly English piece of music in its composition and performance, making its debut not eight miles from Deerhurst, his late grandfather's ancient parish beside the flowing Severn.

George sat in the cathedral yard smoking his pipe. Ralph had told him that the *Fantasia* was a work in progress based on a hymn tune written by Tallis in the middle of the sixteenth century. It would be a bold work, with the orchestra divided into three and placed in different parts of the cathedral to best use the acoustic effect. One of the parts would be a string quartet.

Men and women began drifting into the cathedral through the open south porch. George recognised a young man of about twenty gesturing tensely to a friend as they walked into the cathedral. He was tall to the point of gauntness and wore a shabby flannel suit. His untidy hair flopped over his eyes in a ragged fringe. There was an intensity about this man that made George think that he must be a musician. Perhaps he would seek him out after the performance and exchange a few words with him.

George entered the vast space of the cathedral. It reminded him of one of the major railway stations through which he had travelled. There was a hiss of sibilant speech, which was softened yet magnified by the vaulted roof of the building. He sat down near the back and waited as the orchestra assembled and tuned their instruments. Eventually the audience fell silent and the conductor tapped his baton on the music stand in front of him. The sound echoed round the vast interior before fading into the aisles.

There was no shuffling or coughing as the music soared round the cathedral, building rapidly and fading just as quickly to build again to a crescendo. George was struck by the ghostly echo of the tune by the second part of the orchestra and by how it all came together again before breaking apart and soaring into the vault. He found himself thinking of the scarp slope of the nearby Cotswolds, particularly of the high hills above Winchcombe and Bishop's Cleeve. The music was sublime and he could feel the hairs on the back of his neck tingle.

After just under twenty minutes it was over. There was a profound silence before rapturous applause brought many of the audience to their feet. George noticed the rapt young man almost hopping from foot to foot in ecstasy, his friend unable to restrain him. The applause lasted a long time before the orchestra could perform the rest of the programme.

After the interval George noticed that Ralph had moved to sit beside the intense young man and his friend. From time to time he jotted down notes on his programme.

Following the performance and the prolonged applause, the scraping of chairs indicated that it was time to go. George could have sat happily in the crepuscular vastness until everyone had left but felt obliged to have a word with the young man who had been so moved by Ralph's music. He moved towards the open south door, closing in on the two young men. Bluntly he introduced himself: 'I am George Butterworth, presently studying at the Royal College of Music. I see that you, like myself, were deeply moved by the "Fantasia".'

The young man had the appearance of dried tears on his cheeks. 'I'm very pleased to meet you. My name is Ivor Gurney and I'm hoping to go to the Royal School myself in a year or two. This is my good friend Howler, Herbert Howells.'

'I'd be very happy to offer you my place if I were able to do so. For a composer it isn't all it's cracked up to be, I'm afraid. One must make the best of it, however, and get what one can from it all.'

Gurney could tell that what George was saying to him was deeply meant and wasn't just for effect. He wore wire-rimmed spectacles and had a mouth that George would describe as 'bitter'. But he was friendly, if highly strung, and, above all, sincere. George took to him with his mercurial nature and hoped that their paths would cross again. He noticed that Gurney spoke with a local accent that reminded him of his friend Ralph.

Reluctantly back in London, George felt the return of the restlessness he so often experienced in the metropolis. The Severn plain and the surrounding hills seemed far away both in space and time. He knew that Ralph was working on a piece of music that expressed London in its various moods and was envious. Nothing like that would happen to him; he was entirely dependent on England's rurality for his musical inspiration. He thought of Edward Thomas and his pastoral ramblings. He had heard that Thomas had taken his wife and family to live in a draughty farmhouse in Gloucestershire and that many of his friends were joining him there to write poems, go on long walks and laze around in glorious countryside. He would content himself with outings into Oxfordshire and Sussex, collecting folk songs and dances with Ralph and Cecil. In the meantime, he would plug away at his studies at the Royal College, contain his impatience and eke a living from his father's allowance.

Sir Hubert Parry, Director of the Royal College of Music, had a very high opinion of George. George's technical facility was never called into question but his composition seemed to come in fits and starts. He didn't feel settled enough to be able to concentrate and was experiencing barren periods, which he found disturbing and frustrating.

His organ studies with Sir Walter Parratt and his piano studies with Herbert Sharpe were satisfactory and Charles Wood had a good opinion of his studies in harmony, counterpoint and composition. But after just over a year's study at the Royal College, George became dissatisfied with the music that he was studying and playing.

He was working on composing a series of songs, putting some of Housman's poems to music. The year before going to college he had composed a setting of Shelley's poem *I fear thy kisses*. He was quite pleased with this song, considering that there were no wasted notes in the introduction or accompaniment. It was a good start, but a whole series of Housman poems set to music lay ahead if he could bring himself to complete the work.

Reluctantly George left the Royal College of Music in November 1911. His studies had been far from satisfying and he envied Ralph's brief period in Paris studying under Maurice Ravel. George's restlessness had to be addressed. The answer lay in the revival of the English folk song.

In December 1911 George and Ralph took their bicycles to Norfolk for a few days to collect folk songs. On a clear, frosty night in the Broads they were in a pub when one of the singers suggested that he row the men and their bicycles across a stretch of water to save them a long, dark ride. Halfway across the dark water it became obvious that the rower was drunk. He appeared to be going round in circles. George and Ralph took over the oars and eventually guided the boat to a jetty in the reeds. By this time the rower was fast asleep, and that is how the two men left him, snoring at the bottom of the frosty boat. They rode off to Southwold and were back in the same pub the next evening where their ferryman greeted them like old friends.

Alcoholic excess played a significant part in George's researches into folk songs and morris dances. An old man in Sussex gave a spirited but erratic performance of a song one evening in an inn. George wrote it all down and added notes in the margin to the effect that the old man was drunk and had entirely made it up.

Also in December 1911 a new society for the collection, preservation and performance of the English folk song was formed in St Andrew's Hall, Newman Street, London W1. It was called the English Folk Dance Society and George, who had been on the committee of the Oxford Folk Dance Society since 1911, became an active member of the new society. He served on the committee in the first few years of its existence and worked under its chairman, his friend Cecil Sharp.

Sharp had been collaborating with Mary Neal, who had founded the Esperance Working Girls' Club to promote acting, dancing and music, but they had parted company two years earlier over a difference in ideas and approach. An element of rivalry was to persist for many years between the two societies.

The English Folk Dance Society gave George increased access to the Karpeles sisters, and to Douglas Kennedy, who became a good friend. Things were finally coming together. Sharp's 'School of Morris Dancing' in Chelsea had been running for two years and both Maud and Helen Karpeles had been teachers. They had then founded the 'Folk Dance Club' in their Bayswater home and were instrumental in helping Sharp form the English Folk Dance Society.

George enjoyed the physical side of dancing and was skilled in performing morris dances. He was fit and very coordinated. Soon he was demonstrating new dances and teaching the latest steps. These dances liberated his composition; free from the classroom and lecture hall he could concentrate and banish his restlessness.

While Ralph Vaughan Williams supported the revival of the English folk song movement, Sir Edward Elgar, having shown a brief interest in it in 1899, distanced himself from it, saying that he wished to compose music rather than to collect it.

George was now involved almost every weekend with morris dancing. He was paid a small retainer to demonstrate the steps for the diverse dances from different areas and traditions. He continued with his composition during the week and played a leading part with the week-long courses held at Stratford-upon-Avon at Christmas time and in the summer. In

August 1911 he taught at a month's course there, where he was completely happy, remarking that, for once he had lived in a 'really musical sphere'.

The amassing of folk songs was gathering pace. A few collectors even started to use wax phonographs to record songs. George and Cecil even tried the phonographs themselves on occasions but with limited success. George remained a very non-technical man, being far more interested in art than craft.

In August 1912 another technical innovation was used to further the revival and spread of morris dancing. George's demonstration team was filmed dancing in the High Street in Stratford-upon-Avon. So successful was the filming that the edited result was shown in Pathé's Animated Gazette, the first British newsreel.

A new technique of filming known as Kinora was tried out later in the month at Kelmscott in Oxfordshire. The process was similar to a book of images which, when flicked, produced a convincing moving image. There were demonstrations of morris dances, mainly filmed from the side to show fully all the moves, and an informal performance of a country dance. Each sequence lasted just less than a minute.

The film shows Maud and Helen Karpeles looking lovely in their gym-slips with long dark hair tied neatly back, dancing beautifully together, and with George and Cecil Sharp joining them for a number of dances. All four display every sign of competence and enjoyment. George is wearing a white shirt and dark trousers with crossed baldricks and bells and carries a white handkerchief in each hand. Cecil, the older of the two, wears a light tweed three-piece suit as if he had come along to help out, which indeed he had because the male dancer who would have accompanied George failed to turn up.

The dancing takes place on a mowed lawn in front of a tree with a bare branch emerging from the trunk at right angles, bushes and a hedge, behind which is a glasshouse. It is, at times, so vigorous that George, in particular, disappears momentarily out of the side of the frame to reappear almost immediately. His expression is one of relaxed concentration, serious and somewhat enigmatic. It only changes to a quick look of amusement when he and Cecil briefly collide in the middle of the country dance. George performs one dance on his own, an especially difficult piece that he executes with great precision and quiet enjoyment. One is left wondering if the dances were performed at William Morris's country home at Kelmscott Manor.

George was very much attracted to Maud and Helen. Maud was two years older than he was and very close to Cecil, who employed her as secretary both at home and on his collecting travels. Neither he nor his friend Douglas Kennedy ever speculated on the nature of the relationship feeling, in gentlemanly fashion, that all was innocent and that, in any case, it was none of their business.

Helen was different, a wonderful dancer; she was George's age and unattached. But as time went on it became obvious that she only had eyes for Douglas. George was shy with women, particularly with women to whom he was attracted. Reluctantly he tacitly accorded victory to his friend Douglas and quietly got on with composition and dancing.

The first stage performance of folk dancing in London was on 2 December 1912 at the Savoy Theatre, promoted by Harley Granville Barker. After the second performance, in the evening, George insisted on taking some of the dancers out to a late tea at the Savoy Hotel. The group had not had time to dress properly and were still partly in their dancing clothes. The doorman took one look at the ragged group and suggested to George that the dancers find a cafe on the Strand.

'Right ho,' George replied, fixing the man with a hard look. 'In we go! Come on lads, follow me, I'm your maître d'hôte.' He pushed past the flunkey and held the door open for the group to enter. The doorman looked on, speechless; to make a public scene was more than his job was worth. As the dancers marched into the Savoy tea rooms, George followed them through the door. He turned and fixed the doorman with his eyes once more. 'Thank you. I am, sir, a super-employee of the Savoy. I wish you a very good evening.'

There was something about the intensity of the dark-haired young man with the piercing brown eyes that commanded respect and brooked no refusal. 'Very good, sir,' he murmured weakly. The matter resolved, George caught the waiter's eye and the tired group enjoyed a late tea with hot buttered crumpets.

Despite now considering himself a professional morris dancer, George had been no slouch as a composer. He had quietly begun a number of works during his year at Radley. He constantly revised these early pieces and finally scored them when he considered them ready to be performed. His compositions specialised in two areas: songs and orchestral pieces. He was very much influenced by the English folk songs collected by him and his friends from Sussex, Somerset and East Anglia.

His first orchestral piece performed was *Two English Idylls*, which was played in February 1912 in Oxford Town Hall by the Oxford University Musical Club orchestra conducted by George's old friend and mentor Sir Hugh Allen. The pieces were favourably reviewed by *The Times*. George's overriding feeling was that the harpist had totally ignored his instructions and had played her part exactly as he had told her not to!

Three folk tunes are apparent in the lyrical *First Idyll*, which George succeeded in linking seamlessly together. He was pleased with the performance, apart from the harpist, and also with the critical acclaim.

His next orchestral piece was even more ambitious and contained no folk song tunes, although the *Rhapsody, A Shropshire Lad* was pastoral and lyrical. It was the orchestral culmination of his earlier setting to music of a number of A.E. Housman's poems. It brought to mind the countryside of the Gloucestershire/Worcestershire border. The rounded hump of Bredon Hill with its remote lines of trees near the summit, the contrast with the flatter land of the Severn plain and the steep escarpment of the western Cotswolds was, to George, the absolute essence of rural life in England.

George felt that he had to make a musical record of pastoral England before a possible catastrophe changed it or swept it away. He recalled Housman, a Worcestershire man, looking from afar into neighbouring Shropshire with a romantic but fatalistic eye. For Housman, Shropshire was very much an unknown country, a land of possibilities which would inevitably come to nothing.

George reproduced Housman's protagonist's yearning for a land that he had left, a land that was now lost to him through separation. His view of the countryside was that of a countryman living in London, only able to escape for limited periods of time. *Rhapsody, A Shropshire Lad* was first publicly performed at Leeds Town Hall in October 1913, played by the London Symphony Orchestra and conducted, much to George's satisfaction, by Arthur Nikisch. The applause was rapturous and George had to be pushed on to the stage to take a bow. The critical reviews were generally excellent and many people would remember that they had been present at the first performance of a wonderfully elegiac piece of music.

It was recognised that an important new talent had presented itself in English pastoral composition, a rival to Vaughan Williams and Elgar. George didn't see it in terms of rivalry; he and Ralph continued to get together and discuss each other's works in progress.

George described the *Rhapsody* as an orchestral epilogue to his two sets of *Shropshire Lad* songs with no connection to Housman's words. The two sets of songs had been a success: Six Songs from *A Shropshire Lad* was first performed at a meeting of the Oxford University Music Club with Campbell McInnes singing baritone and George playing the piano. A promising young conductor named Adrian Boult was present and wrote the words of the one song of the cycle not performed, *The Lads in their Hundreds* on his programme. Housman had written this chilling poem about the South African War. Perhaps Boult had a strong feeling of the prophetic nature of the poem and realised that, once again, the clouds of war really were gathering.

In a short space of time George had been recognised as a major new English talent. His natural modesty forbade any resting on his laurels and he continued to revise over and over again everything that he had written.

At the point when life was just beginning to open up at last for George, his beloved mother died, leaving Alexander bereft. George also felt the loss very keenly and went to live for a while with his father in the family home at 19 Cheyne Gardens in Chelsea. George owed a huge debt to his mother; she had taught him much and been a constant encouragement.

But life had to go on. George was increasingly busy and his circle of influential friends widened. Among them was Geoffrey Toye, a young conductor who led the first London performance of *Rhapsody, A Shropshire Lad* in Queen's Hall. On the same occasion Toye conducted the first London performance of *The Banks of Green Willow*, just over a month since its first performance at the Public Hall in West Kirby in Cheshire, conducted then by Adrian Boult.

Another friend was Bevis Ellis, an influential musical promoter who made the Queen's Hall available for the first London performance of the *Rhapsody*. Ellis was also a friend of the composer Arnold Bax who, apart from being an acquaintance of Ellis had nothing musically in common with George. It was Bax who later said: 'A man should try everything except incest and morris dancing.'

One day George went to visit his friend Ralph. He found him in his study surrounded by scores and sheets of music. He was red in the face and uncharacteristically flustered. George sat down on an empty chair and waited. Eventually Ralph put down his pen and peered at George.

'Hello George, good to see you. You might be able to cast some light on to the stew I've got myself into. I'm composing a series of pieces on London and trying to tie them together. It's becoming very complicated and it's started to drive me up the curtain pole. Have a look at it and tell me what you think.'

George took the sheaf of papers carefully in his hand and leafed through them. From time to time he asked Ralph to play some bars on the piano and then went back to his reading. Finally he put the papers down.

'You know, you ought to write a symphony. No doubt about it, the London Symphony. It has all the elements it needs and would make a splendid symphony.'

Ralph looked greatly alarmed. 'That's not it at all! I've never written a proper symphony in my life. Out of the question, dear boy.'

George quietly took his leave and walked briskly home under a smoky London sunset. He knew that he was right but regretted the blunt way in which he had proposed the idea. Time would tell.

The next time he saw Ralph he was surprised by the joy in his face.

'You were quite right, you know. You've resolved the tangle and cut the Gordian knot. *The London Symphony* is beginning to fall into place. It will reflect London in its various moods, sometimes as a busy working city, sometimes as a place for people to enjoy. The changing moods of the place are fascinating and will be drawn together as never before. Will you help me with the scoring and advise me on this work? It is huge, enormous, and will take much time and effort to complete.'

'Of course I will help you Ralph. I'm most honoured to do so. It will do me a lot of good as well. I look forward to working with you very much.'

The next few months were engaged in periods of consultation, of poring over sheets of music with soft leaded pencil and rubber, and of much furious smoking of foul shag in Ralph's study. On numerous occasions the room had to be aired after hours of intensive work. George continued to work hard on his own compositions; the *Bredon Hill* cycle followed the *Six Songs* a year later.

Housman had become a popular man in the musical world. A number of composers were setting his poems to music, matching the human voice to the nostalgia and regret of his poems. They seemed to sum up the spirit of the age: a mixture of heedless actions and paths not taken that resulted in a mood almost of despair.

The villages that nestle against Bredon Hill on all sides are known for the loveliness of their church bells. These bells can be rung for weddings as well as for funerals. They are a commentary on the life and death of fragile man and as such are ambiguous. Whether the bells are sounded for a wedding or a funeral can be arbitrary. Between the villages rises the hill that simply exists in all weathers, an objective entity like the church bells that means different things to different people.

A sound or a note is an objective entity to be combined in a subjective way with other sounds or notes to convey a meaning so intense that an audience is transported to a place far beyond the concert hall.

After one of the many work sessions at Ralph's house he turned to George and said: 'George, a number of us have set Housman's poems to music: Ivor Gurney, you, myself. But I have the distinct impression that Housman thinks most favourably of your work. He spends most of his holidays abroad so we don't see much of him. I am pleased that he feels this and I entirely agree with him.'

'Perhaps my music is beginning to be noticed at last,' George pondered, 'but there is so little of it! How I envy your capacity to work effectively, to compose symphonies, songs, choral music and all sorts. Why does Housman favour me? My accomplishments are modest compared with yours.'

'I am a much older man than you. It took me many years to have anything recognised and, even now, I wonder what is left in me. You have many years ahead of you and so much music in you. Please believe me, dear boy.'

As 1913 turned into 1914 George, then living in Bayswater, went to visit his father in Cheyne Gardens. George felt that Alexander had something to tell him that he somehow felt reticent about. The two men sat in armchairs in the front room in comfortable and companionable silence, before his father finally spoke.

'George, let me be the first to tell you the good news. I have plans to marry again. I have asked Mrs Dorothea Mavor to be my wife. We have a great deal in common and neither of us is getting any younger, although she is thirteen years younger than me. Living alone without your mother has been particularly difficult but that is not the point. Mrs Mavor and I suit each other. She will never take the place of your mother but we very much enjoy each other's company. At present she is in Germany but will return soon and then we shall be married. In a way I must ask for your permission and your blessing. I know how very fond you were of your mother and I do hope that this decision will not go hard with you.'

Sir Alexander lowered his eyes to the carpet and did not raise them again until George spoke.

'Father, I am unreservedly delighted. Thank you for telling me this good news. Your recent letter to me set out your love for Mrs Mavor and your honourable intentions towards her. I presume now that her divorce has come through at last. I don't know why you thought that you needed my permission. You have my wholehearted blessing and congratulations. I look forward very much to meeting Mrs Mavor and getting to know her.'

Sir Alexander breathed a huge sigh of relief. He smiled and stretched in his chair. 'Like yourself I still have much to do. I might have retired from the railway but I have a great interest in the planning of new towns. I want ordinary people to have the chance to live in decent modern houses away from the London slums. They should have the chance to live in pretty towns that are well planned and quiet, places with trees and gardens. Soon we shall move to Hampstead and I shall take long walks on the

Heath with the dogs and think about how life can be improved for the average English families who struggle at the moment in squalid tenements.'

At the back of George's mind was the thought that the years of peace were drawing to a close through no fault of England. It seemed that Germany was beginning to flex its muscles in an increasingly alarming manner. There appeared no end to its bullying of countries closest to it and no restraint to its expansionist ambitions.

Sir Alexander seemed to read his thoughts: 'Germany will be reined in by the strong alliances that have been forged by great powers such as France and Russia, Great Britain and a number of our allies. The kaiser will not dare to move against any of its neighbouring countries for fear of upsetting the delicate balance. It can never win on two or more fronts at the same time despite the bombast and bluster of the kaiser and his generals.'

'Therein lies the danger, Father. We shall be drawn into the quarrels of other nations because of these alliances and Europe will fall like a line of dominoes. The situation in the Balkans is decidedly unstable with Russia hovering in the sidelines waiting for an excuse to release the bear. I do not feel optimistic about the whole situation.'

'Perhaps you have been too much infected with Mr Housman's gloom. When some of the more level heads in charge of the European nations come to their senses and see how much is at stake they will act to prevent a war. There is far too much at stake to squabble over trivialities.'

'Father, I hope you're right. I have to tell you, however, that our country is worth fighting for. I would lay my life down for all that England stands for, for its wonderful past and great future. I do not say this lightly, but if it should come to war I will not just compose English music but will fight for my country.'

'Quite right, my boy. Admirable sentiments. Let's hope and pray, though, that events do not lead to a state of European war.'

Father and son shook hands; each had unburdened himself of a truth that both had initially thought would upset and alarm the other. Each had reassured the other by his loving frankness and, for the moment, all was comparatively right with the world.

Before long Germany had reared its hoary locks in two ways that touched the lives of the Butterworths, father and son.

The long evenings of work on Ralph's *London Symphony* had come to an end. George had played a great part in the scoring of the various sections of the piece and the whole symphony was put in order and written out. There was no time to make a copy because Ralph needed to send the whole thing off to Germany, either to Breitkopf & Härtel, a Leipzig publishing firm, or to Fritz Busch the conductor. This was duly done just before the Archduke Franz Ferdinand and his wife Sophia were shot to death in their car in a side street in Sarajevo by a tubercular student named Gavrilo Princip.

Events moved forward from that point, with Russia mobilising its huge armies in defence of Serbia against Austria. Germany came in on the side of its ally Austria and began to menace the countries that surrounded it. Still Great Britain reckoned that the strong alliance between Russia and France would contain Germany and halt its yearnings for Lebensraum. Then the kaiser confounded them all by invading Belgium and advancing rapidly towards Paris.

Long before the escalation of sinister developments in northern Europe it became obvious that Ralph's precious manuscript would never be coming back to England. As far as Ralph and George were concerned the worst possible thing had just happened. If only they had taken the time to make a clear copy of the symphony.

All was not lost. George threw himself into the huge task of scoring the entire symphony from the rough drafts and scores written for individual instruments. It was a real labour of love and, by the time Germany had invaded Belgium, it was accomplished. Both men were vastly relieved and felt that they had both gained a huge amount by the extra work they had put in on rewriting the complete score.Ralph dedicated the symphony to his friend George.

The other worrying problem was Mrs Mavor's continued presence in Germany. She had gone to take a treatment at a spa at Nauheim, near Wiesbaden. Events had moved too fast for her to come home by train and boat. Sir Alexander and George were desperately worried that she could be interned in Germany or, like the original manuscript of the

London Symphony, simply disappear into the Teutonic forests.

At last a plot was hatched and Mrs Mavor was smuggled across borders into France hidden in the depths of a hay wagon. It was too much for her sensitive nature and she arrived home in a state of nervous prostration. She took to her bed and, even after her marriage to Sir Alexander, lived the delicate life of a semi-invalid. But despite this the marriage of Sir Alexander and Mrs Dorothea Mavor was a happy one, with Butterworth senior devoting his life to the care of his wife yet still finding time to help design Welwyn Garden City and to breed and walk his favourite dogs.

George had to content himself with the company of his close friends. Sometimes they infuriated him. In July 1914 Ralph took the score of *Hugh the Drover* to the home of Sir Hugh Allen at 9 Keble Road in Oxford. George and a mutual friend Henry Ley were present. After a day of playing and singing the 'delightful opera' Ralph suddenly said, 'Will anyone come for a walk?' It was 10.30 at night and Ralph and Dr Ley set off for a long ramble, which went on until six o'clock the next morning. George was left on the doorstep shouting 'Madmen' as they left. One suspects that quite a quantity of alcohol had been consumed.

PART TWO

SOLDIER

Chapter Six

Light Infantry

On 4 August 1914 George was in Stratford-upon-Avon taking part in one of Cecil Sharp's four-week folk music and dancing summer schools. It had just begun and George felt no need to rush madly away to join the Army immediately after the declaration of war. Little Belgium had been violated by the German bully boys. Great Britain had promised to protect Belgium and so was morally obliged to join the escalation of the war. Besides, when Germany had occupied the Belgian and French Channel ports it would inevitably have cast its eagle eye towards the white cliffs of Albion.

George took time to write to his future step-mother, Dorothea, in London. He told her that he would take his time in joining up, would wait for the first surge of national enthusiasm to subside and then make his move. In the meantime, he would finish dancing, demonstrating the morris, and teach it before returning to London to consider his martial future.

Within a couple of weeks he had been offered a commission in the Army by a friend of his father's. He turned it down, writing to Sir Alexander that he considered it wrong to take advantage of private influence at this time. He would join on his own terms and in his own good time.

When George returned to London on 29 August he very quickly found that a group of his friends and colleagues had decided to join up together and remain together. R.O. Morris had gone to his nearest recruiting office at Scotland Yard, where he was advised that the Duke of Cornwall's Light

Infantry had many vacancies in the ranks. Many Cornishmen were in reserved occupations such as mining and fishing and could not be spared for fighting the Hun. Men from London and Birmingham were instead being sent down to the DCLI depot at Bodmin in droves.

George decided to go and join up with this group of like-minded men who were generally older than the average recruit in Kitchener's Army. None were in the Territorials but all wanted passionately to do their bit for king and country. Meanwhile, he went back to Oxford to try for a commission, having made an appointment with an officer from the Officers' Training Corps.

At this meeting the man looked at him gravely and said: 'Mr Butterworth, because you were never in the Officers' Training Corps during your time at Oxford we are unable to recommend you for a commission. My advice to you is that you join in the ranks and then apply for a commission after you have settled in and know what's what. I'm sorry to turn you down but we have to maintain standards.'

'I quite understand, sir,' replied George, taking his leave.

Later George found one of the like-minded friends and the die was cast. There were now eight men who would join the Duke of Cornwall's Light Infantry. There were four musicians of various capacities: R.O. Morris, F.B. Ellis, E.G. Toye and G.S.K. Butterworth. R.A. Ellis, the tallest man in the group at six feet, was the brother of F.B. Ellis; he had come over from British Columbia in Canada where he was a farmer and an engineer. P.A. Brown was a lecturer at Oxford, R.C. Woodhead a civil servant and F.H. Keeling a journalist with a left-wing bent.

There were a number of affairs to be put in order before the train journey to Bodmin. George called round to say goodbye to Ralph. He found him in very good humour. Ralph had just come back from a stay in Margate with his family. While writing notes in the open air for a forthcoming lecture on Purcell he was detained by a Boy Scout who suspected him of being a German spy. Back in London he had just become a sergeant in the Special Constabulary.

George also went to say goodbye to his father on Monday 31 August before reporting to Scotland Yard Recruiting Office with Brown. The two men were told to come back early the next day for the medicals and paperwork. This they duly did and passed the medical examinations with ease. George was very fit from morris dancing and cricket.

Filling in all the papers took a considerable time because of the crowd of recruits surging through the door. In fact over 4,000 men joined the Army on that day. The news from France was bad and men flocked to swell the ranks.

George and Brown were not allowed to leave before they were sworn in and had taken the king's shilling. They were now private soldiers in the DCLI despite having no uniform and kit and no rifle. They were sent away and told to report to Horse Guards Parade at 09.00 hours the next morning, Wednesday 2 September 1914.

The following day the two men presented themselves at the appointed hour. Among the hundreds of men present was the draft for Bodmin, who were assembled and marched off behind a brass band to Charing Cross Underground Station. Eventually they entrained at Paddington, after a hasty lunch, on the 1.30pm train. George found himself thinking that Mr Churchward's crimson lake carriages were not a patch on the old chocolate and cream. He had a soft spot for the Great Western, his father's former employer.

That soft spot was hardening a bit today. There was little room in the train, which was crowded with recruits and soldiers and sailors. He and his friends had to stand in a corridor all the way down to Plymouth. They stretched their legs on the draughty platform of North Road Station before setting off to crawl past the docklands and naval barracks of Devonport. The rhythm of the wheels hollowed as the short train threaded its way under the tubes of the Tamar Bridge into Cornwall, where they were whisked over viaducts, over creeks, through woods and round the sides of steep hills to Bodmin Road Station.

In the dusk the four men carried their bags over a footbridge to a platform where a diminutive engine with two coaches waited for them and the other London and Birmingham recruits to climb aboard. With a hoarse shriek and a sudden bark of exhaust the train lurched off over a viaduct and up a curved gradient. The intervals between the pounding of the rail joints stretched out as the train struggled up the gradient to Bodmin, the county town of Cornwall, where it arrived twenty minutes later.

The men had no time to look at the small terminus of the line. A sergeant formed them into fours and marched them a couple of hundred yards up the hill to a large granite building that looked for all the world like a small German castle. The men entered between what appeared to be a row of stone pigsties leading up to a nailed wooden door, which was flung open by a sentry. Inside the echoing hallway each man was given a blanket and sent upstairs to line up before a high desk. When it was George's turn he was weighed, measured and his chest expansion noted. All the details were written down in longhand by a clerk in a ledger.

Duly attested, the men, clutching their blankets, clattered downstairs to be told that they would have to sleep under a tree behind the building. It was a cold night for early September and various voices could be heard in the accents of Birmingham and London complaining to the sergeant in charge. He explained: 'T'idden my idea to send all you men here directly. The place is full up and you'm lucky to have anywhere at all to sleep.' A phlegmatic man at the best of times, his composure seemed to calm the more excitable men from upcountry.

George and his friends made their way to the crowded dining hall where, after a bit of pushing and shoving, they managed to secure some bottles of beer and a tin of corned beef. Other bottles had been obtained and some of the younger men became a little the worse for wear.

No uniform or kit had been issued and the men had been told not to bring even a change of clothes, so the four new DCLI privates lay down under a tree near a group of increasingly raucous Brummies. One man, apparently from Handsworth, was telling stories of an amazing and unselfconscious lewdness. George remarked that some of the stories were quite funny if they didn't go on for too long. It was hard to sleep on the cold ground under thin and scratchy blankets. From time to time George awoke from a light doze, not quite believing that he was in the Army and in Cornwall. It all seemed unreal; especially when he realised that soon life would be immeasurably harder and more uncomfortable. 'Gather ye rosebuds while ye may' he thought while some toothless man snored nearby.

In the grey morning all the men were stiff and grimy. After a rough breakfast in the dining hall they were ordered outside and made to form fours. Standing to attention they were ordered to parade rest by a sergeant major who addressed the sullen ranks of tired men still dressed in their own clothes.

'Listen up! You men have come to Bodmin! You are the lucky ones! If you go to Bodmin 'tis to join the Army; if you are sent to Bodmin 'tis to attend St Lawrence's Mental Hospital; if you are taken to Bodmin 'tis to the prison with the gallows on the far side of town. So you are the lucky ones! You'm here to become soldiers and become soldiers you will. Sometimes you will not know if you are in the Army, in a loony bin or in prison. Most of you won't be here long. We are very overcrowded and short-staffed. You won't see an officer here before you leave us. Most of you will go to Aldershot for your basic training and then off to France or to Belgium to kill the bloody Hun. What are you in the Army for?'

'To kill the bloody Hun, sir!'

'Good answer lads! I can tell we will get on well. But if one of you puts a foot wrong or pisses me off in any way you will wish you were in a nice snug cell in Bodmin Gaol. Do you understand me lads?'

'Yes sir.'

'I can't bleddy hear a word of that? DO YOU UNDERSTAND ME LADS?'

'YES SIR!'

'That's bleddy better. Now, we'll try to get you some tents for tonight and sort out the cookhouse so that things run a little more smoothly. You'll be issued with uniforms, kit and rifles at Aldershot, which is a bleddy 'orrible place upcountry. But you already know that as most of you lads come from upcountry, poor buggers that you are.'

The rest of the day was spent in drill with the bandy-legged Sergeant Pascoe who had a marked aversion to being addressed as 'Sir'. His rather high voice echoed across the parade ground: 'You will not address me as "Sir". I am not an officer; my parents were married when I was born. I am a sergeant and will be addressed at all times as "Sergeant".'

After the first shambolic drill session there was a medical examination, which was far from thorough. George had been told that Army medical examinations consisted of taking down your trousers and opening your mouth. The medical officer would then look up your backside. If he couldn't see daylight you had passed.

George and his friends were certified fit for basic training and issued with a tent, which they pitched behind the granite depot. It thankfully seemed to be free of the lice that other campers had complained of the previous night. The men were given leave to go into town for the evening.

After twenty-four hours of bemused soldiering, George and his seven friends walked down the hill into town and found the best hotel. There they washed their faces and brushed their clothes before trooping into the dining room and ordering supper. They saw an officer dining at a corner table. He seemed to be amused at the quiet, well-mannered group of men who were enjoying the first decent meal for a couple of days. No contact was made, though, and at the end of the convivial evening, officer and men went their separate ways.

George said to Ellis: 'You know, it seems wrong to be doing this, to be using our comparative wealth to be dining out when most of the chaps can't afford it.'

'In a way you're right. But you can be sure that some of the chaps have spent as much as we have in various pubs and probably haven't been so well behaved.'

George thought that for some of the chaps it was their first taste of a freedom that certainly wouldn't last.

After a chilly night under canvas the eight friends were detailed to entrain once again. They were marched down the short hill to Bodmin General Station and sent off with warrants to Aldershot, a journey that involved no less than three changes, albeit on less crowded trains. Each man wondered why they had been sent down to Bodmin in the first place. But it had been an interesting three days and a good introduction to the organisation of the British Army.

Soon enough the 500 recruits arrived at Aldershot, where they formed fours once more and marched two miles to Watts Common where neat rows of white tents stretched to the horizon of undulating heathland. Tea and a hot meal were issued and the nine friends were put in a tent with two other men, Watts and Coat, 'decent boys of the clerk class' whom they had befriended on the train.

The Duke of Cornwall's Light Infantry consisted at the time of seven battalions of 1,200 men each, each battalion with about 200 men over-strength. George and his friends were placed in the Sixth Battalion. Every battalion consisted mainly of recruits, with a seasoning of regular soldiers, and had four companies; each company had four platoons and each platoon four sections.

Eventually George and friends were in 16th Section, 16th Platoon, D Company, commanded by a major; the other three companies were under the command of captains. Each platoon was led by a lieutenant with a sergeant under him. Sections were under the command of a corporal and a lance corporal.

Sergeant Edmunds of 16th Platoon was a born teacher, 'an excellent man' who was very patient. They were also lucky with Lieutenant Hammond, one of the few officers with any experience. He was quite distant from the men in the ranks having, unlike their platoon sergeant, very little personal contact with them.

Soon they were proficient in basic drill and some quite advanced stuff too. George found drill easy after the discipline of morris dancing and generally enjoyed it. He soon realised that drill was a very effective tool in getting men to obey commands without question. It was hard to drill in ordinary shoes and everyone wondered when they would be issued with boots.

Due to the shortage of officers and NCOs, men were put forward for promotion. Woodhead and Keeling, having had previous training, were promoted to lance corporal, Woodhead becoming 'lance jack' to the section. Toye responded to Major Barnet's call for officers and was accepted, shrinking the group to seven. Nobody grudged him this pro-motion; he had been the last to join the group and seemed to be the right material for an officer, being 'amazingly quick and facile, and full of self-confidence'.

Boots and underclothes were issued, both being a mixed blessing. The brown boots had to be blackened and softened to be wearable, urine being a common softening agent. Best boots, worn only on parade, had to have all grease burned out of them with a candle and had to be polished, or 'bulled', to a mirror-like finish. They were uncomfortable for march-

ing and a major source of blisters. The main problem with the lack of
uniform was having no clothes to change into after a rainy session on
the parade ground. Sitting around in draughty huts and fuggy tents in
damp clothes encouraged cold and influenza. Medical facilities at the
time were almost non-existent.

George described a typical day at Watts Common Camp:

6am. Reveille, dress, clean up tent (a mug of tea is sometimes
obtainable).
7am. Parade – usually a short march along the road.
8am. Breakfast.
9am. Parade – various kinds of drill till 1 o'clock. Half-an-hour is
always given to Swedish exercises [PE].
1pm. Dinner.
2pm. Drill till 5pm.
5pm. Tea. After tea we are liable to be called upon for extra work
any time up to 7pm, but usually nothing particular happens.
7pm – 9.30pm. We are free to go anywhere, and usually go into the
town for shopping and supper.

It is interesting to see that the habit of supper in town, started in Bodmin,
continued at Aldershot; it was a little bit of civilian life after a day of not
particularly strenuous drill and training on the parade ground. Surely
it was not to last.

George bought a Burberry mackintosh because no coats had been issued.
By keeping as warm as possible he managed to avoid the 'flu that Roland
Ellis and then Morris came down with. They were taken to a hotel room
in Aldershot for some reason. George suspected that his group was
perceived as a group apart, potential officer material. In the meantime,
the lack of progress in learning the art of soldiering, put down to a lack
of experienced officers, was becoming frustrating. The battalion was
supposed to be ready to go to France after Christmas but George doubted very much if they would be ready to fight by then. For the time being
they were crowded fourteen to a tent in the blast of a keen east wind.

Inoculation against enteric fever was voluntary; refusal, however, could result in being transferred to the 7th Battalion, which was considered inferior. A visit to a swimming baths was 'an unsavoury business' and pay parade for the company took two hours, with all procedure followed meticulously and tediously to the letter on the blanket-covered table. After receiving his paltry sum of money each soldier was required to say, in a firm voice, 'Money correct sir.' After that there was no comeback.

After a number of depressing and somnolent days in camp recovering from the various effects of the inoculations and sheltering as best they could from the wind and rain of autumn, the 6th Battalion learned that the 7th Battalion was being transferred to a new camp in Woking. All blankets were taken by the departing battalion and horse blankets were issued, rough and smelly and hard to keep clean. A detachment of the Durham Light Infantry were coming to occupy the empty tents.

Khaki jackets and trousers were issued but no caps or puttees were available. Finally proper tactical training began with an eight-mile route march. It was a sunny, windless day but George, being one of the few not yet issued with boots, was forced to remain in camp as orderly, with menial jobs to do and excused all drill.

Next day, rifles having at last been issued, after the first sharp frost of the autumn, a mock attack took place with men advancing fifty yards before lying down and firing as rapidly as possible. It was 23 September and Private Butterworth had been in the Army for just over three weeks.

The thorny question of commissions rose up once again, mainly as a result of boredom and also because a letter received from a General Ovens that day practically offered George a commission in his brigade, the 68th. George had watched Lieutenant Hammond leave, probably destined for France, to be replaced by 'a beardless youth', 'the most incompetent of the lot – who actually had his first lesson in soldiering only a few days ago in the ranks of our platoon'. George was beginning to feel his twenty-nine years of life and experience weighing heavily on him. There were no other commissions available at the time in the DCLI so George talked to his friends and, as Ovens had asked for more men to become officers, it was agreed that the remaining six friends would put themselves forward as a group. Keeling was by now a corporal in the DCLI and Toye on his way to becoming an officer elsewhere.

George suggested that the friends group themselves into pairs 'so that no one would be left alone in the lurch'. George and Morris applied together, as did Brown and Woodhead and the two Ellis brothers.

Consequently, George and F.B. Ellis were given permission to drive over to Pirbright in Ellis's car in order to report to the brigade major. After a nostalgic couple of pints in a pub they arrived at Pirbright Depot at half-past four in the afternoon to find a vast camp of four battalions with nobody in uniform. The two men were directed to the brigade major's tent, guarded by 'a seedy Tynesider with a two-day's beard; an intensely comic picture'. The major, a very relaxed 'dug out', knew very little and had had no communication with General Ovens. He intimated that there were commissions available but that there were no vacancies for second lieutenants. However, he thought that lieutenancies and even captaincies were there for the asking and he promised to let the men know what came up in a day or two. George found himself thinking that the DCLI was quite a tight ship by comparison. Both men agreed that they had experienced a most unmilitary afternoon.

Back at Watts Common the weather improved and days were sunny and nights frosty. George was disgusted with the corruption and extortion practised by the cooks, who passed a hat round for 'improvement in the rations'. He also considered that the night guards were very slack and slap happy; he was unconsciously beginning to think like an officer. He was present at the visit of King George V, who came to inspect the camp where the whole division presented arms on the Queen's Parade Ground, a 'futile proceeding' with no band.

The splendid weather continued and, after three weeks in the tented camp, George decided that the life of a private soldier was all physical, with no thoughts of the outside world or the bigger picture of the war. Reports of casualties trickled through to the camp, reminding the men that things were happening a couple of hundred miles away in France and Belgium.

Nothing was heard from General Ovens or the brigade major and Army bureaucracy continued to grind good men into the ground. Eventually, news of the friends' impending commissions came from Ovens, subject to permission from the DCLI. It was promised then rescinded, the

DCLI claiming that the men had previously been offered commissions by them. This might have been so individually but not en bloc. General Ovens stuck to his guns and got permission for the six men to leave the DCLI after a week of car journeys to and from Pirbright Depot with messages and representations.

The general really asserted himself and the six men were called from parade on his orders. He ordered them to report to Bullswater Camp as soon as possible. This cut through the face-saving tactics of the DCLI. An hour or so later the six future officers were on their way with all their kit in Ellis's car and a taxi, shaking the proverbial dust of the DCLI from their feet. They left Lieutenant Toye and Sergeant Keeling behind. It was 15 November and they reported to General Ovens who received them most cordially, if delivering a setback.

'Bit of a cock-up, really. While all the faffing around was going on some of the vacancies were filled. Now the War Office says there are no vacancies even though I know that there are. I cannot appoint you without their blessing, so the best thing is for you all to go to town, get yourselves kitted out and in decent uniforms and stay at home until called back for training. There will be vacancies as more officers are sent to the front.'

George found it very discouraging to take a step backwards after five weeks' training. Now he would be at home sitting idle at the whim of the War Office when there was a war on. This was another example of the Army's philosophy of 'festina lente' (make haste slowly).

Once back in London George went to Moss Bros in Bedford Street, WC. Here he was fitted for an officer's uniform by 'their Mr Peter' who was 'especially wonderful': 'he threw things incontinently on my back, they just stuck there, and fitted beautifully'. With an officer's uniform and kit allowance of only £30, George chose economy over class, rejecting the higher prices charged by Pope and Bradley of Bond Street and Humphrey and Crook in the Haymarket. As a second lieutenant George would be paid 5s 3d a day with a further 1s 6d towards mess bills. As the New Army gathered strength and numbers, Kitchener raised the daily rate to 7s 6d with 2s 6d for foreign service. Most officers banked at Cox and Co. at 16 Charing Cross, London.

George had to buy two dress service jackets, a Sam Browne belt and sword, shirts, ties, breeches, service cap, leather knee boots, brown shoes, revolver, sweater, underclothes and socks. He was to look neat but not gaudy; overdressed officers were known as 'Nuts' and were looked down on by their fellow officers. George would have to avoid excessive mess bills and live fairly frugally. But he was used to this way of life and to him it would prove no hardship. He was about to become a 'temporary officer' and was a little surprised to find that the different items comprising his uniform were all different shades of green and khaki. He was to find that this state of affairs was common and appeared not to matter.

London was gloomy place in late 1914. There was a blackout in place because of the threat of Zeppelin raids and the streets were depressingly dark at night. George was fairly happy to live back with his father and his new wife but felt guilty that he was not leading a more active life. 'Civilian anxieties' about the progress of the war returned and George read Bernhardi's book *Germany and the Next War*, which made him think that 'Germany's crime is primarily an intellectual one – too much theory – the doctrine of the end justifying the means is wrong, because it's impossible to prophesy accurately what either will be.'

At last George and his five friends became officers. F.B. Ellis and R.A. Ellis became first lieutenants in the 10th Battalion, Northumberland Fusiliers; R.C. Woodhead a first lieutenant in the 10th Battalion in the Durham Light Infantry; and P.A. Brown, R.O. Morris, and George Sainton Kaye Butterworth second lieutenants in the 13th Battalion Durham Light Infantry.

Brown, Morris and Kaye Butterworth had been originally appointed first lieutenants but 'as the 13th Durham's [sic] had been particularly strong in junior officers, Brown, Morris and self requested to be made seconds'. There were two things of note here. Firstly, George would be known from now on as Kaye Butterworth, bearing the surnames as an officer of both sides of his English family. Secondly, he was anxious not to be promoted above his experience. Bearing in mind the sorry spectacle of the 'beardless youth' proving ignorant of drill and missing the target ten shots in a row in the close-quarter range, George determined to take his time and learn his trade thoroughly. He wanted very much to be a good and competent officer who would be effective in the field and in battle against the enemy.

Before reporting back to the Army George had one more thing to do. He went through his papers and manuscripts and decided what should remain and what should not. On to the living room fire went many early compositions and all the work that he did not consider worth keeping. Should he return from the war perhaps he would compose more and better work. If he did not, then he did not wish to be remembered for music that did not come up to the standard of his best work. There was no vanity in this decision; just a clearing out of what George considered clutter. His father noticed what he was doing and came into the room.

'Dear boy, what are you doing? Do you want to deprive us of your wonderful music? Please stop what you are doing before it is all gone.'

'I am sorting out the dross that is of no further use. There is enough of my music to remember me by. When, or if, I return from the war, I might well compose more music.'

'George, I want you to know how very much we appreciate and enjoy your wonderful pieces. Your decision not to become a man of the law was the right one. It took me some time to learn that. You could say that the boy became the father of the man. We are very proud of you and our prayers will go with you when you go back to the Army to become an officer.'

'Thank you Father, you know that I have to go and fight in this war. I cannot leave it to others. All my friends are going and I must go too. This country of England is worth it. The last few years have shown me that. It is because of my work, my composing, collecting and dancing that I know that, to the core of my being, this is so. I knew that you would understand, Father.'

'It took me long enough, I'm afraid. This dancing business I've never really understood. Tell me, George, what is the difference between morris dancing and country dancing? It all comes from rural England does it not?'

'Indeed it does, Father. Country dancing is more widespread and is performed by men and women together. It is commonplace and is done for fun, for the joy of the thing. Anyone may perform it at any time. There are regional variations and some country dances are more ancient than others.

Morris dancing is only normally performed by men and is a professional matter. Every team has a bagman who passes the hat around. Morris teams may be hired for a specific event or celebration. In order to become a morris dancer a lot of fitness and dexterity is required. It is not for everybody. One has to undergo extensive training for several weeks and be judged fit to dance.

A morris dance is a ceremony to mark specific events or the passing of the seasons. It is not just performed for pleasure, although a successful morris dance is a great pleasure to perform. One comes away with a sense of achievement, rather like when a squad in the Army has been drilled to precision on the drill square. A morris dance connects us to events long past in England, it's a serious business which can be enjoyed if it goes well. It also has great regional variation, even from parish to parish. In this respect it is a little like a country dance.'

'Thank you for putting it so clearly. I begin to understand your enthusiasm and your enjoyment. And I fully agree with you that this country has a huge amount to offer and is worth fighting for. I am very proud that you are about to become an officer in the Durhams and have no doubt that you will become a very good one.'

The two men looked at each other in silence. Neither man wanted to be the first to speak and to raise the spectre that had risen between them. What would it be like if George, the beloved only son, the talented composer, the continuation of the Butterworth line, never came home from the war?

Back at Bullswater Camp George settled in quickly as a second lieutenant. He felt that he had, at last, found his place in the Army. He was a subaltern, a subordinate to higher authority. But he was encouraged to use his mind in a way that a private soldier was never expected to do. He had a future, however small, in the direction of the war. With ability he could rise and command more men than the 11th Platoon, most of whom were splendid Durham miners who applied themselves with great ability and enthusiasm and often with a valid questioning of authority. George found that the majority of officers and NCOs lacked experience and, consequently, authority. Self-confidence was lacking, especially among the recently promoted NCOs; George found that after five weeks of training with the DCLI that he still knew more than most of his sergeants. This was Kitchener's New Army, men from the Regular Army were few and far between. They were busy fighting in France and were regarded as 'contemptible' by the kaiser because of their lack of numbers.

Bullswater Camp consisted of about 350 tents, on dust in summer and mud in winter. Officers slept two to a tent and large marquees were used for canteens and recreation.

With George in command of 11th Platoon and Morris leading 10th Platoon, training proceeded smoothly. The company had a full complement of officers who got on well together. The commanding officer of 13th Battalion was Colonel Ashby, 'a distinguished soldier who fought at Tel-el-Kebir'. The second in command was Major Biddulph, another retired regular officer.

George continued to have a great admiration and affection for the men who were 'above all, Northerners'. He understood and appreciated them and they, in their turn, valued him for his faith and trust in them. Life in training wasn't easy. With hardly any flat ground to drill on or open country to practise movements on, things were restricted. Good equipment was not to be had, and rifles were of an obsolete pattern and only good for drill. The autumn wind rose, heralding the approach of winter. Tents and marquees blew down and the temperature plunged to twenty degrees of frost, making life under canvas miserable. A movement to Malplaquet Barracks was announced for 16 November, then cancelled, and actually took place on the last day of November. The brigade packed up its now wet tents and blankets for the move to Aldershot. General Ovens was judged to be too old for service in France and duly retired.

During the period in camp, when the rain was constant and life in tents miserable, nobody complained. As George put it: 'It is to be hoped that those who grumble at national slackness of the working people will make an exception in favour of the working people of Durham County; the large majority of these men have given up good jobs and comfortable homes for the best reasons, and are willing to stand almost anything, if only they are allowed to get out and finish off the war.'

Any trace of class consciousness or snobbery that George might have held had been dispelled by his intense respect for the men under him in the Durham Light Infantry. His upbringing had not previously exposed him to the quality of the common man and he was quick to acknowledge that the Army was making an egalitarian of him. That process had begun with his appreciation of the dances and folk songs of the working people of England.

The brigade left Bullswater Camp in the driving rain, grateful to be moving to a hutted camp. Over a hundred lorries and traction engines moved most of the soaking kit to Malplaquet Barracks. A party was left behind to dismantle and move the tents when the rain finally stopped. The wind blew hard as the main party left at about midday in advance of the tents. Comfortable barrack rooms with fires in each awaited the swearing, soggy men and their officers when they arrived at Aldershot.

The momentous year of 1914 finished in a stalemate between the kaiser's army and the decimated French Army and British 'contemptible little army', the latter a force of only 250,000 professional soldiers compared to the kaiser's 3.8 million. The Germans had come close to Paris and had been forced back from the River Marne by the brute force and mad determination of the French and British Armies. Trenches had been dug by both sides from the Belgian coast to the Swiss frontier. The French Army held the majority of the front with their excellent artillery and infantry 'élan'. The British held the northern part of the front from Belgium's flooded coastal marshlands, down past the Ypres salient into France, deep into Picardy and the uplands of the Somme.

George's platoon now had a full complement of uniform and kit and were snug in their warm huts. They felt more like soldiers as their confidence in their training grew.

In May 1915 George and his platoon, now well trained and very fit, were transferred from Aldershot to a new company at Bramshott in Hampshire. He suddenly found himself as temporary second in command and then temporary company commander in charge of 240 men whom he scarcely knew by sight. He wrote in a letter home: 'This is likely to continue perhaps for a fortnight, and involves immensely complicated accounts and considerably more responsibility than is good for any one at such short notice. However, I hope to pull through!'

Bramshott proved to be the last billet for George in England, and also the best. The men were billeted in huts with straw mattresses and 'the whole business is more like active service than anything we have done yet'. The camp held the 68th and 69th Brigades and was sited just to the south of the Portsmouth Road. The officers' quarters had a fine view down a valley with a good view of a railway line. Indeed, everyone must have felt now that all roads led to France.

Officers could go to 'Mrs B's cottage' for a bath and dinner from time to time. The rifles and ammunition had not yet been issued so the road to France was still temporarily barred. George and his fellow officers had stopped going out to supper in the evening at the caterer's mess and drew ordinary Army rations which, supplemented by food bought in, was cooked by 'our own soldier cooks'. They ate well and saved money, living much better than they had at Watts Common or Bullswater.

George found out that his cousin Hugh, successfully established as a teacher at a boys' school at Wanganui on the North island of New Zealand, had left his post to come back to England and become an Army officer. He had been very happy and popular at Wanganui Collegiate School, had scored some wonderful runs at cricket, but had been called back to the old country by the war. Hugh had taught at Wanganui from the autumn of 1907 and left at the end of the autumn term in 1914. He was accepted for a commission in the 9th (Service) Battalion of the Rifle Brigade and his training period was much shorter than George's.

In May 1915 Second Lieutenant Hugh Montagu Butterworth embarked for France with his brigade under the grudging command of Lieutenant-Colonel Charles Villiers-Stuart, who had a low opinion of 'schoolmaster' officers. The CO was a good officer but a remote figure who would later be given cause to regret his hasty view of schoolmasters.

Before he left for France Hugh had his photograph taken in Aldershot in his tailored officer's service dress. He looked slightly strained and uncharacteristically remote. His younger sister Irene was unnerved by the photograph, saying that it made him look 'almost a stranger' and 'too much the sort of advertisement for the British Army'. Hugh's Army career was to be quite short but remarkably distinguished.

On Wednesday 25 August 1915 the fairly recently promoted Lieutenant George Kaye Butterworth (now paid no less than 8s 6d a day plus his 2s 6d field service allowance), now commanding the 2nd Platoon of A Company, was sent to France with his brigade. He had become senior subaltern and, for over a month, had been acting company commander at Bramshott. He was now one of the older junior officers, having turned thirty in July. Little did George know that his favourite cousin Hugh had but exactly a month to live.

Before leaving for France, the 23rd Division had been inspected once more by King George V. Officers on leave were recalled and there was a feeling that, at last, something momentous was about to happen. The review took place in open country between Guildford and Haslemere and did not just consist of the king walking down the long ranks of men. George considered the review a fine sight 'and the moment when the King, at the head of his train, galloped into sight through a defile in the hills, was quite thrilling'.

The brigade was embarked very quickly on to ships and crossed the Channel with a one-destroyer escort on a fine and windless night. They arrived in France early on the morning of 26 August, marched a few miles to camp and spent the rest of the day settling in and resting. To an officer 'resting' was a misnomer. There were numbers to be checked, kit to be accounted for and, above all, the welfare of the soldiers to be seen to. The old cavalry motto to the effect that the horses were to be fed first, the men second and the officers last was taken very seriously by a young subaltern who was yet to experience action against the enemy.

The 'resting' didn't last very long. In the middle of the night everyone had to get up, collect their kit and march to a railway station. There the soldiers waited for over two hours while over fifty trains passed, heading mostly away from the front. George was fond of trains but even he was tired of locomotives with empty carriages rattling past in the wrong direction. Eventually the right train arrived; the officers climbed into three first-class compartments while the men squeezed into cattle trucks forty at a time.

The train did not take them to the front, though. It was the usual case of 'hurry up and wait'. After arriving at a small wayside station a French interpreter took charge of them and marched them five hot miles to a village in the direction of Armentières where billets were provided: farm-houses for officers, barns for the men.

At last the percussion of the heavy guns could be heard. George reckoned that they were about forty miles from the front. Life was generally very quiet for a week, with less to do than when they were at Bramshott. They felt like spectators watching heavy traffic and 'scorching dispatch riders' on their way to the British headquarters.

George noticed that, although the countryside was not unlike England, the people were subdued and greeted the Army with no enthusiasm. They were cooperative and businesslike but had no illusions that the war was going to end soon.

One of George's main tasks was censoring the men's letters home. He had to make sure that no soldier revealed where they were or what was happening. Most of the men were bewildered by their lack of under-standing of the French language. They asked constantly for Woodbines, which cost 1d a packet, because they couldn't get on with French cigarettes.

At last, on 6 September, the brigade formed up and marched twenty miles. It was a longer and more gruelling march than anything attempted up to that point. The cobbled roads, heavy packs and the heat took their toll. One in ten of the men fell out and straggled into camp and their billets long after the main column. Next day they marched a further fifteen miles and half the brigade fell out with blisters and heatstroke.

The brigade was now 'within five or six miles of the front' and the crack of individual rifle shots could be clearly heard. The following day there was an inspection by the general commanding the Army Corps and the brigade was informed that it would be sent by platoon up to the front to spend twenty-four hours in the trenches with the companies serving there 'for instructional purposes'. Each platoon would have two days in and two days out before further training and then take up their own positions in two or three weeks' time.

By 18 September George and his platoon had been in the trenches at Sailly-sur-la-Lys for three twenty-four hour periods of observation. It was in a 'quiet' section of the front near Armentières; there was the 'evening hate' when the artillery opened up as the sun went down. By then George and his platoon were following a guide along a communication trench that approached the front line at right angles. The guides were frequently confused and tired and often led the platoon up blind alleys. After turning back and swearing volubly the platoon eventually arrived at the fire trench which lay about 600 yards along the communication trench. The occasional crack of bullets flying overhead took some getting used to but George felt perfectly safe in the deep trench.

The first difference that George noticed about the front-line trench was that, unlike the trenches dug for practice, it zig-zagged every few yards, presenting from the air a saw-toothed appearance. The second difference was the presence of breast works, built up from sand bags in front of and behind the trench. Also, he observed that 'immediately opposite the entrance I found, to my astonishment, a little wooded shanty, and the officers of the company having dinner; so at the moment when I felt braced up for a vigorous onslaught on the Hun, I was hauled off to roast beef and beer, while the sergeant posted the men'.

As the artillery barrage died down, rifle shots continued the 'hate' and flares were fired into the air every minute or so. George discovered that it was much safer in the trench than in a working party behind the lines where stray bullets and shells occasionally hit unlucky men. Firing was much more intense at night because of the possibility of fighting and reconnaissance patrols being sent out from both sides under cover of darkness. There would be bursts of machine-gun fire that went on for as much as half a minute and kept everyone's heads down. From time to time wiring parties would go out to mend the rolls of barbed wire that were placed directly in front of the trenches and that were frequently damaged and moved by artillery fire. No matter what kind of patrol was sent out it was always under the command of an officer, who would be the obvious target for German snipers or machine gunners.

Because George had no particular duties in the fire trench he slept very well and soon became accustomed to the rattle of rifle fire at night.

During the day life was much quieter, with all observation of the enemy 500 yards away viewed through periscopes. George had the distinct impression that the Germans were ahead in the tricks of trench warfare, about even as regards machine guns, and inferior in artillery.

After three separate periods of observation George's platoon sustained no casualties and only experienced the nearby explosion of one enemy shell. They saw no Germans and no dead or wounded men. Altogether, the battalion had twelve men wounded, five by enemy machine-gun fire on the way home from the trench, and the rest hurt in a mine explosion.

George and his platoon spent time in divisional reserve four miles behind the front, expecting to be sent to their own trench in a week's time. They were not entirely safe from the German heavy guns and could hear the artillery from both sides firing at each other for half-hour periods. George sent two letters home to his father to whom he referred as 'the General', insisting that none of what he had written should make it into print. He assured everyone at home that he was safe and well and in very little danger. He was unhappy to hear that London had been raided at night by Zeppelins but considered that the danger was small compared to life in France.

While George and his platoon were held behind the line in reserve, his cousin Hugh was getting ready for the Battle of Loos. Hugh was thirty miles north of Loos, just a few kilometres north-east of Ypres, and was to be part of the northern diversion to the battle that came to be known as the Second Attack on Bellewaarde.

Hugh was a very promising officer. Aged twenty-nine, he was a year younger than George and held a similar rank, lieutenant, in the 9th (Service) Battalion of the Rifle Brigade. He commanded D Company and was one of only fifteen unwounded officers left in the battalion. The commanding officer, Lieutenant Colonel Villiers-Stuart, had come to value his subalterns and especially the 'schoolmaster'. These subalterns, in their turn, trusted the CO implicitly, appreciated his excellent organisation, and felt that he worried inordinately about their safety.

He had every cause to do so. The attack, although meant to be diversionary, was against all the odds. Hugh would be attacking an entrenched enemy with well-dug-in machine-gun nests and excellent fields of fire.

It was going to be 'a relentless tough fight'.

Hugh had been in action several times, had found it terrifying and exhilarating by turns. He described himself in action commanding his company as 'half on the parapet and half on the parados [with one foot on each side of the top of the trench] with a revolver in one hand and a rifle near the other and a cigarette going well, using the most unquotable language. Do you know that really was a good moment.'

Several days before leading his men into battle for the last time, Hugh wrote a letter to his friend John Allen, a fellow schoolmaster at Wanganui. It is headed 'Belgium, September, 1915' and stares his imminent death in the face:

> I am leaving this in the hands of the transport officer, and if I get knocked out, he will send it to you. We are going into the big thing. It will be my pleasant duty to leap lightly over the parapet and lead D company over the delectable confusion of old trenches, crump holes, barbed wire, that lies between us and the Bosche, and take a portion of his front line. Quo facto I shall then proceed to bomb down various communication trenches and take his second line. In the unlikely event of my being alive by then I shall dig in like blazes and if God is good, stop the Bosche counterattack, which will come in an hour or two. …Unless we get more officers before the show, I am practically bound to be outed as I shall have to lead all these things myself. Anyway if I do go out I shall do so amidst such a scene of blood and iron as even this war has rarely witnessed.

A few days later Hugh totally vanished, leading D Company into an attack on the German positions between Railway Wood and Bellewaarde Farm. The ground he had to cover was exactly as he had described it in his last letter except that it was raked by machine-gun and rifle fire and then saturated by shell fire from the 'Bosche' batteries. No trace of Hugh or of his fellow company commanders was ever found. It is possible that he was atomised by an exploding shell or buried in the upheaval of the barrage. His name can be found on Sir Reginald Blomfield's magnificent Menin Gate memorial in Ypres (Ieper).

Hugh had a great deal in common with his cousin George. Both men shared a wry sense of humour and an ability to face the facts head on. Hugh, who bore a resemblance to his 'Uncle Alik', George's father, was the more outgoing of the two and much more of an extrovert than George. Both loved playing cricket and ball games. Both led from the front and fully faced their responsibilities, outstanding Army officers with a deep respect and fondness for the men under their command. And both loved their country and were determined to face up to the German bullies.

On the day his cousin was killed in Belgium in the Battle of Loos, 'the big push' began for George. After two days of heavy bombardment of the German trenches, George's battalion was marched seven miles to a 'certain town' where they were billeted and held there as corps reserve, ready to be sent to where they were most needed.

In early October George and his battalion were chosen to relieve the 12th Battalion of the DLI in their trench. Life was even quieter in the trench than it had been when they were observing. They had a busy time, even so, constantly repairing the 'trenches', which were, in fact, breast-works, built-up walls of sandbags rather than deep excavations due to the high water table. Because that part of the front was practically at sea level they had to be fashioned upwards rather than dug down. The front line had been there for a year and required continual maintenance. Behind it was formed a 'conglomeration of passages and cross walls; the geography of these is worthy of the maze at Hampton Court, and in striking contrast to the neat regularity of trenches built for training purposes'.

Junior officers had very little sleep in the trenches. Most of the work and fighting was done at night. Sentries had to be posted and checked at regular intervals. Occasionally they could be snatched by German patrols and taken back to their lines for interrogation. The wire in front of the forward trench had to be repaired and extended on a routine basis. It was generally safer in the trench at night. Despite spasmodic firing from the German lines and the odd short burst of machine-gun fire George reckoned that 'one could quite happily eat one's supper on the parapet, provided one retired below for one's smoke!'. The secret was to keep quite still when flares were sent up. During the day life was much more dangerous. George wrote, prophetically as it turned out:

On the other hand, by day it is usually (though not always) extremely dangerous to expose even the top of one's head for more than two or three seconds. A German sniper, even at 400 yards, can make pretty good practice at a six inch target, and we have already lost an officer and one or two men in that way. Moreover they frequently crawl out at night and take up a position from which by day they can pot away at our parapet without fear of detection. Of course it is the telescopic rifle that does it, and it is curious that the authorities do not think that it is worthwhile to put us on equality in this respect. But in reality this sniping business is more of a nuisance than a danger, and it is quite unnecessary for anyone to expose himself by day, and by night the sniper can do nothing much.

George was, at the time, writing as a fresh young officer who had not yet been subjected to prolonged artillery bombardments, weeks of little sleep, and the constant attrition of cold, wet, mud and death.

During the day, forms were to be filled in, letters censored, reports written, orders taken and passed on, together with a myriad of small, intricate tasks such as daily inspection of feet, rifles and kit, and the early morning issue of the rum ration. The Navy rum came in heavy earthenware jars marked 'SRD' for Special Rations Department. It had to be issued by an officer, was extremely strong, and was generally put into tea, which often tasted of the petrol that had been in the cans before they were used to carry water.

Even in late October the weather that year was dry, although increasingly cold. Flying biting insects were dying down, although fleas and lice were unaffected by the autumn chill. Also impervious were the ubiquitous trench rats. They were brown or black rats which, having grown fat from feasting on corpses shallowly buried or thrown up by shell fire, skittered around the trenches and dugouts at night, ran over the slumbering men and kicked empty cans around to see if they contained anything to eat. The French Army were universally and unfairly blamed for burying their dead too shallowly, and the rats grew fat, sleek and increasingly bold, running over the faces of sleeping men and eating their rations and parts of their kit. The approved method of killing a rat by placing a square of cheese on a fixed bayonet and then firing one's rifle was soon dispensed with in favour of battering with a brick or stabbing with a bayonet.

George also spent a lot of the daylight hours supervising the bringing up of supplies through the numerous communications trenches that wound their way between the front-line trenches and the rear areas with their dumps of ammunition, rations and kit. He managed about six hours' sleep out of every twenty-four. This he considered to be not too bad.

One night two men volunteered to go out into no man's land under cover of darkness to try to kill some of the German snipers who had been making trench life unpleasant for days. When they failed to return after a reasonable interval, George volunteered to go out the next night with one other officer and fourteen men to find the missing soldiers. Because of the constant but sporadic firing from the enemy trenches the assumption was that both men could be lying wounded out in the open. So under cover of darkness George followed the rescue party 'over the bags' into no man's land. He soon took lead of the patrol after an alarming incident in which one of the men threw a grenade at a tree that George was convinced concealed a German soldier. After the bright flash and explosion there was no retaliation so the patrol carried cautiously on through the ragged wire and round the shell holes.

For an hour and a half they crawled, wet and tired. George found that he was growing impatient and urged the men on at a faster pace, but no sign of the two soldiers was found. Eventually the patrol turned back and, after a while, stood up and walked briskly towards the British trenches. All attempts at concealment were abandoned and there was no retaliation from the German side. As George put it: 'Casualties nil. Results, ditto, except some experience and amusement.' The scouting party had been very lucky and George recognised that it had been the

George Sainton Kaye Butterworth. *Bodleian Museum, Oxford*

The Reverend George Butterworth at Deerhurst Church, Gloucestershire. *Kathi Green*

3 Driffield Terrace, The Mount, York. A back view of the Butterworth house, third from right. *Carter Jonas, York*

George Butterworth (centre) at Eton.
Bodleian Library, Oxford

George Butterworth, (up mast), with R. O. Morris (left), on Sir Hugh Allen's boat, around 1907.
Bodleian Library, Oxford

English Folk Dance Society group at Stratford-upon-Avon, 1914. Helen Karpeles (extreme left), Cecil Sharp (centre), Maud Karpeles (two over to right of Sharp), George Butterworth (extreme right). *Bodleian Library, Oxford*

(Above) Five men from EDFS Morris Side at Burford showing crossed sticks logo. Left to right: James Paterson, George Butterworth, A. Claude Wright, George Jerrard Wilkinson, Douglas Kennedy. *Bodleian Library Oxford*

(Right) A Country Dance at EDFS Summer Festival at Stratford–upon-Avon, 1914. Left to right: George Butterworth, James Paterson, Maud Karpeles, Helen Karpeles. *Bodleian Library, Oxford*

EDFS Morris Side dancing at Kelmscott. Left to right: Perceval (correct spelling) Lucas,?, George Butterworth,?, A Claude Wright, George Jerrard Wilkinson. Butterworth, Wilkinson and Lucas were all killed in the Great War, as was Reginald Tiddy (not shown). *Bodleian Library, Oxford*

EDFS group at Stratford-upon-Avon, August 1914 with Butterworth's handwriting above. This photo shows GB with rumpled white shirt, striped jacket with upturned collar and pipe identical to his portrait smoking pipe wrongly shown as 1911. *Bodleian Library, Oxford*

George Butterworth's attestation papers as a Private in the Duke of Cornwall's Light Infantry, filled out in London, 1 September 1914. *Public Record Office, Kew*

Description of *George Butterworth* on Enlistment

Apparent Age _29_ years _____ months.	Distinctive marks, and marks indicating congenital peculiarities or previous disease.
(To be determined according to the instructions given in the Regulations for Army Medical Service.)	(Should the Medical Officer be of opinion that the recruit has served before, he will, unless the man acknowledges to any previous service, attach a slip to that effect, for the information of the approving Officer.)
Height _5_ feet _9½_ inches.	
Weight _147_ lbs.	
Chest measurement { Girth when fully expanded _37½_ inches. Range of expansion _33_ inches.	*Scar in back*
Complexion _fresh_	
Eyes _brown_	
Hair _brown_	

Religious denomination:
- Church of England _Yes._
- Presbyterian
- Wesleyan
- Baptist or Congregationalist
- Other Protestants (Denomination to be stated.)
- Roman Catholic
- Jewish

Certificate of Medical Examination.

I have examined the above-named man and find that he does not present any of the causes of rejection specified in the Regulations for the Army Medical Services.

He can see at the required distance with either eye : his heart and lungs are healthy : he has the free use of his joints and limbs, and he declares that he is not subject to fits of any description.

I consider him * _fit_ for the Army.

Date _1st Sept_ 191_4_

Place _London_

* Insert here "fit" or "unfit."

Note.—Should the Medical Officer consider the Recruit unfit, he will fill in the foregoing Certificate only in the case of those who have been attested, and will briefly state below the cause of unfitness :—

_____

Medical Officer.

Certificate of Primary Military Examination.

I hereby certify that the above-named recruit was inspected by me and I consider him * _fit_ for service in the† _Duke of Cornwalls Light Infantry_ and that due care has been exercised in his enlistment.

Date _Sept 1st_ 191_4_ . _McBrien Major_

Place _London_

* Insert here "fit" or "unfit." † Insert the "Regiment" or "Corps."

Recruiting Officer.

* Certificate of Approving Officer.

I certify that this Attestation of the above-named recruit is correct, and properly filled up, and that the required forms appear to have been complied with, I accordingly approve, and appoint him to the† _Duke of Cornwalls Light Infantry_

If enlisted by special authority, Army Form B. 203 (or other authority for the enlistment) will be attached to the *original* attestation.

Date _Sept 1_ 191_4_ . _McBrien Major_

Place _London_

* The signature of the Approving Officer is to be affixed in the presence of the Recruit. † Here insert the "Corps" for which the Recruit has been enlisted.

Approving Officer.

George Butterworth's attestation papers, September 1914. *Public Record Office, Kew*

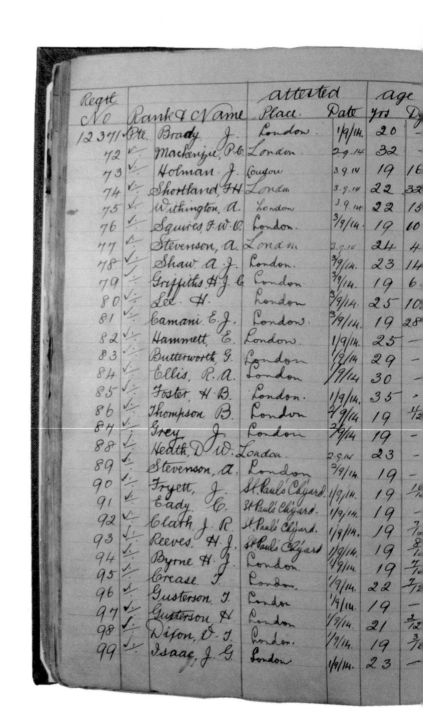

Regtl No	Rank & Name	attested Place.	Date	age yrs	Dy
12 371	Pte. Brady. J.	London.	1/9/14.	20	-
72	Mackenzie, P.C.	London.	2.9.14	32	
73	Holman. J.	London	3.9.14	19	16
74	Shortland, F.H.	London	3.9.14	22	32
75	Withington, A.	London	3.9.14	22	13
76	Squires, F.W.O.	London.	3/9/14	19	10
77	Stevenson, A.	London	3.9.14	24	4
78	Shaw A. J.	London.	3/9/14.	23	14
79	Griffiths H.J. C	London.	3/9/14.	19	6.
80	Lee. H.	London	3/9/14.	25	10
81	Camani. E. J.	London.	3/9/14.	19	28
82	Hammett. E.	London.	1/9/14.	25	-
83	Butterworth, G.	London	1/9/14	29	-
84	Ellis, R. A.	London	1/9/14	30	-
85	Foster, H.B.	London.	1/9/14.	35	-
86	Thompson B.	London	1/9/14	19	4/12
87	Grey J.	London	1/9/14	19	
88	Heath, D. W.	London.	2.9.14	23	-
89	Stevenson, A.	London	3/9/14.	19	
90	Fryett, J.	St. Pauls Chyard.	1/9/14.	19	1/2
91	Eady C.	St. Pauls Chyard.	1/9/14.	19	-
92	Clath. J. R.	St. Pauls Chyard.	1/9/14.	19	7/10
93	Reeves. H. J.	St. Pauls Chyard	1/9/14.	19	8/10
94	Byrne H. J.	London.	1/9/14	19	7/10
95	Crease J.	London.	1/9/14.	22	7/12
96	Gusterson. J.	London	1/9/14.	19	-
97	Gusterson H	London	1/9/14	21	3/12
98	Dixon, D. J.	London.	1/9/14.	19	3/10
99	Isaac, J. G.	London	1/9/14.	23	-

Entry dated 3 September 1914 for Pte Butterworth, G and Pte Ellis, R A, reporting for training at DCLI Depot, Bodmin. *Duke of Cornwall Light Infantry Museum, Bodmin*

Height. ft. ins.		Weight	Chest min max		Religion	Remarks
						Rebel
						1st Battn
5	5½	122 lbs.	31½	34	C of E	Falmouth
5	5	122.	32½	35	C of E.	Falmouth
5	6½	150	34½	37.	R.C	Falmouth
5.	6½.	120.	32½	35,	C. of E.	Falmouth
						1st Battn
5.	8½.	124.	33½	35½	C of E.	Falmouth
5.	5½.	120.	32	34½	C. of E.	Falmouth
5.	9.	160.	36.	38½	C of E.	Falmouth
5.	9½.	140.	35½	38.	C of E.	Falmouth
5.	9¼.	147.	34	37½	C of E.	
6.	0.	175.	37½	41.	C. of E.	
5.	8.	135.	32	34½	Presb.	
5.	11.	154.	34½	38½	not stated	Malta
5.	6½.	126.	31½	35.	C of E,	
5	6¾	135.	34.	37.	C of E.	
5.	3½.	118.	34	36	C of E.	
5.	5¾.	124.	33	37½	C of E.	
5.	5.	124.	37.	39.	C of E.	
5.	8½.	120.	32	34	C of E.	

Trench map of Contalmaison, Somme, showing OG 1 and OG2, the new Switch Line, Butterworth
Trench and Munster Alley, July 1916. Butterworth was killed close to the number 61 just below the
'M' of Munster Alley on the map. Bailiff Wood is in the middle of the map at the bottom.
Public Record Office, Kew

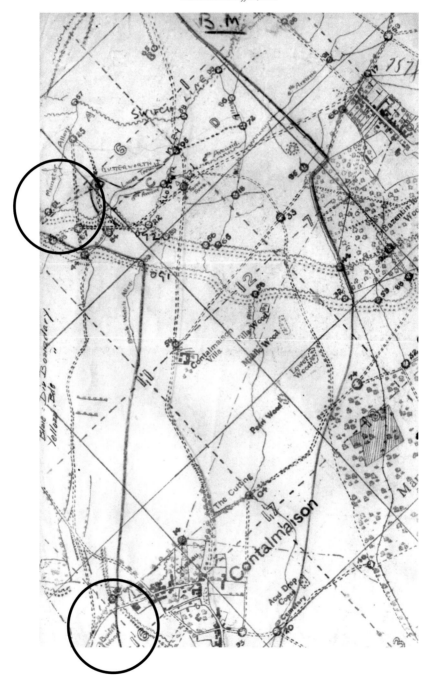

DIARY.

REPORT ON OPERATIONS UNDERTAKEN BY THE 13TH D.L.I. ON
NIGHT OF AUGUST 4/5/8/1916.

The attack was launched in two waves, the leading wave
advancing from NEW TRENCH at 9.16 p.m.   They immediately came
under rifle fire from TORR TRENCH and machine gun fire from behind
the Barricade in MUNSTER ALLEY.

The second wave followed 50 yards behind and some men under
Captain AUSTIN obtained a footing in TORR TRENCH where a bomb fight
remained in progress until about 2.15 a.m.

After the second wave crossed MUNSTER ALLEY a strong party
bombed up MUNSTER ALLEY for about 80 yards, where they were stopped
by a block which was wired, held by the enemy with a machine gun
about 40 yards S.W. of Point 73.   A block was made from which we
were later compelled to fall back a few yards to another block.   This
block was about 18 yards from that of the enemy.

At 12.30 a.m. the exact situation was ascertained.   A second
attack was not launched as the watchfulness of the enemy and enfilade
machine gun fire from MUNSTER ALLEY (where a hand bomb fight was in
progress) rendered it unlikely that fresh troops would be able to
cross MUNSTER ALLEY without becoming disorganised.   A party was
at once sent up MUNSTER ALLEY to try and drive the enemy away from
behind his block.   At 2.30 a.m. this was reported to have failed and
so another party was organised and sent up to try another attempt.
By 3.15 a.m. most of this party had become casualties so about 20 men
were sent to hold the block in MUNSTER ALLEY.

(Above) Diary entry for 4 and 5 August 1916 recording the fighting in Munster Alley immediately before Butterworth's death. (Below) Stained War Diary entry for 13th Bn. Durham Light Infantry describing heavy fighting in Munster Alley immediately before Butterworth's death.
Public Record Office, Kew

			WAR DIARi. *or* **INTELLIGENCE SUMMARY** *(Erase heading not required.)*	Army Form C. 2118
Instructions regarding War Diaries and Intelligence Summaries are contained in F. S. Regs., Part II. and the Staff Manual respectively. Title Pages will be prepared in manuscript.				
Place	Date	Hour	Summary of Events and Information	Remarks and references to Appendices
TRENCHES N.E. of CONTRE MAISON	Aug 4th		13th D.L.I relieved 10th N.F. during the morning in the front line 2 Coys 10th N.F. remaining in front System under orders of O.C. 13th D.L.I. Enemy artillery fire very severe between 4 a.m. and 6 a.m. Our artillery carried out intense bombardments at 1 a.m. and 6 a.m. at 7 P.M. a continuous bombardment of enemy's system was carried out lasting until 9 15 P.m. when 2 mins intense bombardment took place. at 9 15 P.M. D coy 13th D.L.I. attacked MUNSTER ALLEY and TORR trench to the west of MUNSTER ALLEY. jumping off from NEW Trench In cooperation B coy 13th D.L.I bombed up MUNSTER ALLEY from x56 4.1. frontal attack failed but a bomb post was established 120 yds up MUNSTER ALLEY. Enemy artillery fire very heavy throughout the night	

Telegram 31 July 1916 informing that George Butterworth was injured on 28 July. *Public Record Office, Kew*

Telegram 9 August 1916 informing that George Butterworth had been killed in action. *Public Record Office, Kew*

Telegram 18 August 1916 informing that 'Lieut G S Kaye Butterworth Durham Light Infantry was wounded 27 July but remained at duty and was killed in action 5 August 1916.' *Public Record Office, Kew*

Lieut. G. S. Kaye Butterworth killed in Action.

It is with deep regret that we record the death of LIEUT. G. S. KAYE BUTTERWORTH, M.C., only son of Sir A. Kaye Butterworth, General Manager of the N.E.R. Lieutenant Butterworth fell in action on August 5, 1916, after leading a bombing party to a successful attack on an enemy trench. Only a week previous he had been slightly wounded, and for his work during the strenuous fighting of July had gained the Military Cross. Unfortunately, he did not live to receive the notification of this honour, the news being conveyed to Sir Alexander Butterworth in the following letter dated August 8 :—

" The Commanding Officer wishes me to write to you and inform you that the Commander - in - Chief has awarded to your son the Military Cross.

" This was awarded him for the very excellent work he did during July. He again earned the Cross on the night of his death, and the great regret of the Commanding Officer and all his fellow-officers is that your son did not live long enough to know that his pluck and ability as a Company Commander had received some reward."

A later communication enclosed the purple and white ribbon of the decoration and contained this brief official account of the circumstances under which the award was made :—

" *Lieutenant G. S. K. Butterworth, at Pozières, from 17th to 19th July, 1916, commanded the company, of which his captain had been wounded, with great ability and coolness. By his energy and total disregard of personal safety, he got his men to accomplish a good piece of work in linking up the front line.*

" *I have already brought forward this officer's*

Lieut. G. S. Kaye Butterworth, M.C.

name for his work during the period from the 7th to the 10th July, 1916."

Lieutenant Butterworth, who was born on July 12, 1885, was educated at Eton and Trinity College, Oxford, and from a very early age evinced great musical talent. One of his compositions was played at an Eton school concert while he was still a boy there. Among his musical publications are two cycles of songs from Housman's " Shropshire Lad," and an orchestral rhapsody, which was played at the last Leeds Festival and also at Queen's Hall in the spring of 1914. He devoted much time to the collection and arrangement of folk songs and folk dances in collaboration with Mr. Cecil Sharpe, and took an active part in the formation and in the work of the Folk Dance Society. He also contributed musical criticism to *The Times* intermittently for several years, and a biographical notice which appeared in that paper on August 12, contained the following appreciation :—

". . . whatever he wrote showed shrewd judgment, sound knowledge, and independence of view. He was, in fact, a musician of great promise as well as a man of sterling character, who, if he had not given his life in a greater cause, would undoubtedly have done much to further a national ideal of musical art in this country."

Immediately war was declared, Mr. Butterworth, like many other brave spirits, left all else and enlisted as a private soldier in the Duke of Cornwall's Light Infantry. After a time he was offered and accepted a commission in one of the Service battalions of the Durham Light Infantry. He left for the front on August 25, 1915.

How keen was his interest in his duties may be

George Butterworth's obituary in the North Eastern Railway Magazine, August 1916.
National Railway Museum, York

(Above left) Grave of Pte. F. Strickland, A Company, 13th Battalion, Durham Light Infantry, Ovillers
Military Cemetery, Somme. (Above right) Bailiff Wood, Contalmaison, Somme, 5 August 2016.
Hugh Butterworth, George's first cousin, left, the author, right. *Kathi Green*

Distant view of Bailiff Wood, Contalmaison, Somme, 5 August 2016. *Kathi Green*

(Above) Hugh Butterworth and Anthea Ionides Goldsmith, great grand-daughter of Sir Alexander Butterworth's second wife, Pozières Town Hall, Somme, 7 August 2016. (Right) Anthea Ionides Goldsmith beside the Mayor of Contalmaison at the Centenary Commemoration, Butterworth Farm, Pozières, Somme, 7 August 2016. *Kathi Green*

Where George Butterworth was killed. Torr Trench is a few yards behind, and parallel to, the road. It joined Munster Alley at right angle, near Pozières, Somme, on D73, August 2016. *Kathi Green*

CWGC Monument, Chemin de Butterworth, Butterworth Farm, Pozières, Somme. *Steve Darlow*

Great War Monument, St Peter's College, Radley, Oxon. *Kathi Green*

Inscription on CWGC monument, Chemin de Butterworth, Butterworth Farm, Pozières, Somme.
Steve Darlow

way not to conduct a patrol.

But there was a happy ending to the experience. The next day the two dirty, weary missing men returned to their dugout. They had approached the German trench in daylight and killed a couple of men before lying concealed until nightfall. On their way back to their own trench they encountered a patrol – very possibly George's rescue party, although in the darkness they had no way of knowing if it was the enemy – and lay still, cut off from their own lines. When the sun came up they found a shallow trench that led to the British trenches and slowly and laboriously crawled up it before arriving after thirty-six hours out in the open.

Between duty in the trenches George was resting behind the lines in fairly comfortable billets. He had no great sense of achievement from his time in action. He was learning the ropes and now had time to reflect on his experiences. Officers' billets were usually superior to those of the men. Most officers took turns as billeting officer and it took a fair amount of diplomacy and skill to place officers and men in comfortable temporary homes. French householders and farmers were paid five francs a night for officers and one franc for soldiers. Officers sometimes ended up sleeping in beds, or at least on mattresses, while privates and NCOs had to make the best of hay and straw in barns.

By the beginning of November George 'had done practically nothing but eat, sleep and play chess' in 'the most frightfully dull country imaginable'. It had started to rain and every day it poured incessantly, turning the ground to mud. George knew that after his return to the trenches life would be very different.

In the meantime, the five officers in D Company messed together, combining food parcels from home with the regular Army rations to which they were entitled. George received, and shared, 'a rather splendid parcel from D[orothea], rather extravagantly large'.

After another largely uneventful spell in the trenches, George was sent on a bombing course. For eight days he was taught how to throw Mills bombs, hand grenades recently developed for 'bombing up' enemy trenches. These grenades were neat and reliable, unlike earlier bombs made of jam tins and grenades with faulty fuses. They were easy to throw. George, who was a keen cricketer, found that he could throw a bomb a good twenty-five yards with reasonable accuracy. This was hopefully farther than an enemy soldier could throw the heavier German 'potato masher' stick grenade.

Mills bombs were 'segmented for easy fragmentation'. 'And what does that mean Private Perkins? Like a bleedin' chocolate bar.' The segments acted like the shrapnel balls in shells and would kill and maim at considerable distance from the explosion of the grenade, whose impact would be made worse by the confinement of the narrow trenches.

George was soon aware that one of the great problems would be keeping the men supplied with bombs. It would be all very well reaching the enemy trench with a bombing party, but to run out of bombs would be a disaster. He was also aware that he was in no danger from enemy action on the course, but that bombs were dangerous toys.

Back with the battalion the mud was all-pervasive. It covered George's trench coat, adding considerably to its weight. 'In short we are getting some idea of what a winter campaign really is,' he commented.

A very bad item of news was that Lieutenant P.A. Brown, 12th Battalion DLI, had been killed. He was in front of the trench parapet when he was ambushed by a German patrol. The soldier who was with him managed to carry him back to the dugout but Brown died of his wound on the way to the dressing station. He was the first of the eight 'pals' to die, but by no means the last.

After another few days in the trenches George found that he was due some leave. He planned a few days at home towards the end of January. The time at the front had been cold but otherwise uneventful; frostbite had been avoided.

On 9 December George wrote home from a convalescent home with a 'chill'. What sent him there must have been something a little more serious but George, in his letters home, did not want to alarm his father and future stepmother. Life was dull but comfortable. George had the chance to read a book for the first time for months. In the trenches he had no time or concentration for anything more than newspapers or *Punch*.

By 13 December he was back in the trenches. He wrote home to say that he didn't need the armour plating that his father had promised him.

He knew that nothing would stop a shell or a bullet fired from a reasonable distance; he would therefore take the same chances as the men.

The year closed with the momentous news of a Victoria Cross awarded to Private Thomas Kenny, 13th Battalion DLI. It was the first VC won by the regiment in the war and was a very similar story to that of Lieutenant Brown. Private Kenny was a Durham miner of the self-sufficient type greatly admired by George. On 4 November near La Houssoie, Armentières, Kenny's officer, Lieutenant P. A. Brown, George's friend, was shot through both thighs while leading a patrol in thick fog at night. Private Kenny carried Brown back to the British trench while under fire from German machine guns, rifles and grenades. He put him down in a safe trench and fetched the company commander, Captain White, leading him back to Brown despite his exhaustion. Brown was taken to a forward dressing station but died on the way, probably from loss of blood. Such was the devotion of the soldier to his wounded officer; there would be many more examples of selfless heroism of this sort.

The year 1915 finished fairly quietly on the Western Front. Winter was setting in on a year of momentous events. Gas had been used for the first time by the Germans at Saint-Julien near Ypres. The *Lusitania* had been sunk off the southern Irish coast with heavy loss of life. Yet another 'big push', the Battle of Loos, had fizzled out with negligible gain to the Allies. The war of attrition against an entrenched enemy on generally higher ground, in better-constructed trenches and dugouts, continued. Surely the new year of 1916 would lead to a new initiative to bring the war to an end?

On 22 January 1916 Lieutenant George Kaye Butterworth left the Armentières area for eight days hard-earned leave at home. He left a flat, desolate landscape scattered with conical spoil heaps from numerous coal mines, long streets of depressing brick houses, and a population worn down by a war that seemed to go on and on with no progress. Winter was a grim time in industrial Pas de Calais.

George sat alone on the torn seat of a grimy green French railway carriage rattling and jerking across a bleak winter landscape. A keen wind whistled through the broken glass of the grimy window and George pulled his filthy trench coat up to his ears. He would have to have his hair cut and clothes washed before turning up at 16 Frognal Gardens, Hampstead. He hoped to do this at Boulogne while waiting for a boat to England.

Eventually he arrived in Boulogne after sitting in numerous sidings waiting for trains passing in the opposite direction. The main flow of traffic seemed to be eastwards at last. Boulogne appeared as tired and as wintry as towns closer to the front. But here good food and a bath in a decent hotel were available, as well as a calm walk round the top of the high walls of the Old Town. A haircut and moustache trim also freshened George up. He was glad to be alone at last, not hearing the impact of the guns and the crack of rifle fire.

Nearly everywhere he went in the town he saw wounded men, some French some British. Apart from the sight of bandaged and haggard soldiers, life was fairly normal in a subdued sort of way. The occasional pretty girl smiled at George in passing, seeing a handsome young officer, a little careworn, with luxuriant brown hair and a fine moustache. They saw a man in his prime, upright and confident yet at the same time shy and deeply reserved. Even the prostitutes sensed that the man before them was content to be left alone.

For his part George was happy just to smile absently back and to tip his field service cap to women young and old. Inside, he was very pleased to be back in a world where women were everywhere, where it was normal not just to see men and trenches.

His dark mood lifting, George looked down from the walls at the Cimetière Nord. Alleys of white gravel bisected rows of grey and white family tombs decorated by crosses, broken columns and angels reaching towards the grey sky. In one far corner he couldn't help noticing ranks of white wooden crosses and khaki-clad figures filling in a grave. The tiny figures were far away but they reminded George that there was no way that he would be able to escape the war even when at home in London. Resigned, he knew that, until the war ended, his life would be in suspension. There would be no music, no composition, no dancing; but he would continue to fight for the England that had made it all possible. He had no regrets; he realised that he actually rather liked the

Army despite the slowness, the tediousness and the apparent futility of life in the trenches.

Looking towards the grey Channel George saw the smoke on the horizon of a grey paddle steamer approaching the port of Boulogne. It was time to collect his laundry and make his way down to the quay.

Chapter Seven

Hampstead and back to France

The train journey from Dover to London reminded George that England was virtually untouched by the war. The countryside was beginning to waken after a wet winter. Greening fields and orchards flashed past the intact window of the speeding train. The sky was clearing and the occasional church tower and oast house could momentarily be seen. Primroses starred the banks and violets briefly lifted their heads as the train passed.

Even grimy old London was a welcome sight. The train rumbled across the bridge into Victoria Station and came to a halt beside a long platform filled with men in khaki and nurses in long blue dresses. George was amused to see the cleanness and newness of the uniforms but soon saw bandaged men on stretchers waiting in rows to be collected and taken to various hospitals. If one were sent home with a 'Blighty one', George reflected, the first feeling would be of immense relief. One's platoon or company would no longer depend on one, a huge responsibility would be lifted. But, soon enough, the feelings of emptiness would come; one would be letting down all the men who normally depended on one. It would be a complex business being wounded. A blue serge uniform would replace the khaki one. What about the pain and the loss of body parts and function? It hardly bore thinking about!

Hampstead was far enough away from the roar and clatter of London to be almost rural. On rising ground with the Heath not far away it seemed the ideal place for living. The house in Frognal Gardens was new to George and he liked it. It was warm and comfortable and far from the war.

The first evening that George spent with his father was very pleasant. Because Sir Alexander and Dorothea were to be very soon married, the bride to be was staying in another house until the wedding ceremony. George and his father were alone once more with a feeling of companionship as they sat in front of the fire, the curtains drawn and the pipes lit.

'George, I'm delighted that you're here for my wedding to dear Dotty. She's a fragile flower but I will have the time to look after her here. We'll take walks on the Heath with the dogs and live a very pleasant life together, one of great companionship.

This war cannot end quickly enough. Surely something significant must happen this year to end it. We regret very much dear Hugh's death but know that he did not die in vain. He gave his life for his country and, dare I say it, for the Empire. He could have so easily stayed in New Zealand but chose to do his duty for us all. Just as you are doing. It isn't easy for us old buffers back home. We cannot play our part in the fighting like you young men. All we can do is wait, hope and pray that it will all come out right.'

'But, Father, you and Dotty do a great deal by sending food parcels, magazines, socks and warm underclothes. We share all these things and that make us feel that we are not alone in the trenches. We feel valued and supported. Thank you from the bottom of my heart.'

'And we very much value the letters you send home. Obviously you cannot tell us where you are or what's really going on. But just to know that you are alive and well is most reassuring. When we don't hear from you for a while we know that things have hotted up. I know you spare us the details but we still worry about what you are going through. Hugh's letters were much more revealing than yours. He went into great detail about the actions he took part in. In a way I'm glad you don't do that. I know that if you did it would worry Dotty very much. I would also have sleepless nights. But I can't help feeling curious about what the war is really like.'

'Well, Father, a lot of the time we're cold, bored, filthy, itchy and cross.

But we can't think of ourselves for too long. What makes the whole shooting match worthwhile is the care and direction of the men under us. They really are splendid fellows, able and used to thinking for themselves. Most of them are miners; they are tough and stand no nonsense from Fritz. They really keep me going and are the reason why I am out there. To me and my fellow officers they represent what is best about England. Often, as they go about their duties, I hear them singing to themselves. From time to time I even get the chance to write down some of the words and the tunes. But I'm afraid this doesn't happen very often.

We find that we don't actively hate the Germans. We hate what they do. Most of them are there because they have no choice. The German NCOs and some of the officers are the ones we dislike. We spend our time trying to kill them because they spend their time trying to kill us. We don't want to live in a world run by the kaiser. It's hard to think of him cradling the dear late queen on her deathbed. His vision of Europe is not good and his militaristic ambitions must be stopped.'

'George, my boy, it's very difficult for us to imagine you at the front. It was very hard for me to fathom what you did as a composer. Your late mother, bless her, had a much better understanding of it. And I think that Dotty has too. But I know that composition and music is right for you. And I feel that the Army suits you too, in a peculiar way that is very real. Parents are not always destined to understand their children but more to appreciate them and what they do. It has to be enough.'

'You're absolutely right, Father. Without your trust and support I could not have achieved anything at all that really matters.'

'Oh yes! That reminds me. I found out the other day that you were nearly asked to write the music for Blake's *Jerusalem*. If Sir Hubert Parry hadn't been able to take it on he suggested that you were the man for the job.'

'I'm glad Sir Hubert is doing it. I would have had great difficulty in finding the time. He will make a very good job of it and will do it in much less time than I could have done.'

As the two men sat in companionable silence Sir Alexander found himself trying to reconcile a shy and sensitive man, who had composed some beautiful pieces of music, with an Army officer who killed the enemy and decisively ordered men to go into harm's way. His only son was turning out to be a much more complex person than he had even considered.

George went to see his friend Ralph before his leave was up. He found Ralph's wife and children at home and was far from surprised when he learned that Ralph was in France. His wife sat him down, gave him a cup of tea and told him, with great pride, that Ralph had joined the Royal Army Medical Corps not long after George had reported to Bodmin. At the age of forty-two he had gone off to France as a private to drive an ambulance, taking wounded men from close behind the front line to hospitals farther back. It was demanding and dangerous work and George felt proud of his friend for making such a sacrifice when he could easily have stayed home in London. He hoped that he would be able to see Ralph soon, perhaps on his next period of leave in England.

The wedding between Sir Alexander and Dorothea was quiet and, as befitted a wartime wedding, subdued in its celebrations. George enjoyed the ceremony and wished the couple well for the future; she had been very kind and attentive to him, sending him food parcels, socks and other necessities for his use in the trenches. He was glad that his father had found a companion to care for and to care for him. He was still a very active man, with many ideas for the betterment of humankind. The idea of new towns with lawns, gardens, trees and decent housing would be the way forward for a nation picking itself up after the cessation of the interminable war. It was still only an idea but one that was growing in Sir Alex's mind, as well as in the minds of other people who took a longer view than that of the war.

Leave was over soon enough. George was somehow eager to get back to the front, to the men under his command and to the eventual completion of the task in hand. It could take years; experience of the war so far showed that nothing would happen quickly or even soon. But an initiative would have to be taken at some point. Attrition would only result in stalemate. Surely the big push would happen sometime during the summer of 1916.

George set off for France in his second-best uniform, stained and invisibly mended but clean and pressed. His Sam Browne belt no longer creaked and no longer held the glossy shine of newness. The two stars on his lower sleeves were faded and a little frayed. His regiment didn't go in for 'funk jackets', tunics with the stars on the shoulder straps. His brown knee boots were polished and many of the scratches no longer showed. His breeches were stained at the knees and skilfully sewn up where they had been torn by barbed wire. His field service cap was somewhat crumpled where the stiffeners had broken. Badges, collar dogs and buttons were highly polished for the time being. Gas had the propensity to turn brass a horrible greenish hue.

He had also learned that the pale young man whom he had met in Gloucester Cathedral had also joined the Army. Ivor Gurney was now a private in the Gloucestershire Regiment serving somewhere on the Somme. George wondered how he was dealing with life in the trenches, the filth all around and the sight and smell of death. Gurney had seemed somehow fragile despite the passion burning inside him for music and poetry. Pray God that he would not become another case of 'shell shock' or victim of a self-inflicted wound. But George thought that he would be all right if the Germans didn't kill him. Were he in George's platoon he would be trusted and steadfast, definitely not a man to get 'windy'. Perhaps after the war the real problems would begin: the nightmares, disorientation, delusions. George wished him well from the bottom of his heart.

George looked what he was, a competent and experienced front-line officer, a platoon commander in a good regiment in the British Army. He represented England, a country for which he was offering to lay down his life.

After a foggy Channel crossing and a pleasant, but expensive, day spent in Boulogne, George reported back and was sent on a course in signalling. Because communications between trenches and between the front and headquarters were increasingly important, they could not be left to the experts. George was taught Morse code, how to repair a cable and how to run a line across broken country. By the end of the course he knew exactly how a telephone worked as well as a myriad of technical information associated with communications. He felt rather proud of himself for being so technical and for having understood matters that he had previously considered beyond his ken. The hutted accommodation offered by the course had also kept him out of some particularly foul weather.

He went back to corps reserve duties. He wondered when he would be given the chance to signal with flags and heliograph lamps that reflected the rays of an often absent sun to distant points.

Soon afterwards, intense fighting began in the French sector far to the south at Verdun. Conditions were worse than before and plans were made for a diversionary attack in the north to take the pressure off the beleaguered French who were dying in their thousands for no appreciable gain, despite newspaper reports that all was going well. Lieutenant Kaye Butterworth had the distinct feeling that soon he would be involved in some real fighting, not just maintaining a trench in the face of relentless enemy opposition, but hacking and gouging hand-to-hand.

George hoped that he could do it. He had no hate in his heart but a huge indignation against the stupidity that had caused this interminable stalemate. He was back in France to defend the country that meant so much to him. But he would fight for his men and his brother officers, he would experience fear but would try his hardest not to show it. The worst thing that could happen would be a loss of nerve, a 'funk', for which he could never forgive himself for putting his own skin above that of the loyal men with whom he was fighting the 'Hun'.

Back in billets George was glad to see his fellow officers. They were generally younger than he but, although forming no intimate friendships, he got on well with them. He knew that they could be killed or posted to other battalions with no warning so he made no close attachments. They saw him as a reserved man who tended to speak his mind, a man a little apart, not unfriendly but slightly remote as if the greater part of his life lay far away from the battlefield. He was seen as a very good officer, never hasty in making decisions but slow and careful. Once his mind was made up to a particular course of action he would follow it relentlessly to its conclusion.

The NCOs and men saw him as a dependable and caring officer who always had a word for them, saw to their well-being before his own, and was in possession of a good sense of humour and a keen sense of the ridiculous. He was a quiet man, never a show-off, who believed in encouragement. Often a disapproving look from his dark eyes would have a greater effect than words. He would tend to be amused by the strangest things. Nothing was known about his life in the civilian pre-war days. It was rumoured that he was keen on music. He often noted down the words and tunes sung by the Durham men who had worked down the pit. Yes, he was absolutely an officer worth following.

George saw tough men of small stature, many looking old beyond their years. They were used to thinking for themselves and didn't always take kindly to discipline imposed by thoughtless men. But George knew that if they trusted you they would follow you anywhere. They spoke in a lilting, almost Scandinavian, way that George found musical. They were grimy and worn, their tired eyes looked quizzically from tanned and seamed faces. These were the men of Durham, proud of their mining craft and darned good soldiers. Used to looking after each other down the pit, they had the instinct for survival that transcended self-preservation. Captain George White had come to the rescue of the dying Lieutenant Brown, brought back from no man's land under intense fire by Private Kenny, VC. As George's company commander he knew as well as George the quality and loyalty of these men of Durham.

As winter gave way to a chilly spring the battalion had moved to the sort of mining country familiar to many of the soldiers. Conical spoil heaps and brick rows of houses dominated the landscape. Long streets of semi-rural aspect with neat allotments – 'jardins ouvriers' – brick factories and horses in small, grimy fields made the men of County Durham feel quite at home.

Soon a march to the south brought the battalion to rising chalk uplands that made George think of the Sussex downland. As he set about his billeting duties he unconsciously hummed parts of *The Banks of Green Willow*.

A brother officer walked up to him and said: 'George, what is that tune? It's somehow familiar from a concert I went to before the war. It makes me think of home, of the English countryside far from this damned war.'

'I believe it's called *The Banks of Green Willow*. It's quite a recent piece by a largely unknown English composer.'

'That's a curious title. I tend to think of willow in clumps or hedges rather than banks.'

George felt himself drawn into the discussion. His natural modesty forbade any revelation of who composed the piece. 'From what I remember the banks are underwater. There are elements of an old Sussex folk song in the piece. A servant girl and her lover ran away to sea after stealing some money from the house where they worked. A baby was born on the voyage but mother and child soon died. They were thrown overboard into the banks of green willow, an area of the ocean, where the long tendrils of seaweed waved in the current like willow in the wind.'

'You know a lot about this, George. Do you know who composed the piece?'

'I ought to know but the name escapes me. I've always been interested in collecting old folk songs and stories from rural England before they vanish forever.'

'I envy you that interest. I have noticed that you sometimes note down tunes and words sung by some of the men. Anything that takes the mind away from dwelling on this war is good.'

George turned away with a nod and walked into a barn to kick the straw and count the rats. He wondered why he didn't want to reveal the fact that he was a composer; most of the time he could hardly believe it himself. Music seemed quite out of place in the trenches, where raucous songs of increasingly cynical gloom enlivened marches and boring times of waiting. There was little of beauty in the ravaged landscape of the front.

Taking one's turn as billeting officer could be tedious and frustrating. George found that he rather enjoyed finding temporary homes for the battalion. There was a certain satisfaction in seeing officers and men relax for a short time in reasonable comfort. He didn't mind arguing with farmers and householders who were trying to get a better deal; he understood their desperation. He firmly believed that the British Army were making a difference and doing a good job. Unlike many other soldiers he also believed that the French Army was effective and that they were also doing the best they could.

He generally felt that the senior officers in both armies were competent and had only cynical feelings about a number of politicians back home who were not pulling their weight in the struggle to victory. As reported by the press, things were going fairly well at Verdun and George considered that the Germans could only sustain one more large offensive. He had the feeling that the 'big push' could be coming soon.

Life in billets was pleasant but very temporary. As usual 'rest' meant strenuous exercise and manoeuvres behind the lines. Men seldom had a chance to lie or sit around or to think too much about what was going to happen next. Often marches towards the front line were halted and reversed because the situation had changed. The battalion sometimes found itself back where they had started from. Soldiers' sense of irony became highly developed by what they considered the vagaries of staff or senior officers. Junior officers such as George were often no better informed but were kept frantically busy looking after the needs of their men. At least, thought George, intense activity passed the time quickly and gave one the chance to talk to people.

After a sudden fall of snow spring seemed far away. Fortunately the battalion was still in billets and relatively warm and comfortable. George had just finished shaving when Lieutenant Target walked up to him. He peered into his face before saying:

'I see you're managing to keep that moustache under control. You know that you're the envy of some of the younger subalterns who can barely manage to grow a "nelly nine-hairs".'

'Yes, I'm quite attached to this 'tache. When this war is over I'll be able to let it grow out again. It won't matter by then if it does frighten the horses.'

'I wonder what the world will be like when we've won the war. Unlike your moustache it'll take a long time for everything to get back to normal. Will there be enough jobs for the soldiers when they return home? Will the strikes continue as they were before hostilities? What shall we do with all the cases of shell shock? What will become of men like you?'

'Men like me, Target? What do they do and how are we different?'

'I must confess I think I've rumbled you, Butterworth. Remember the air you were humming the other day? *The Banks of Green Willow* I believe it was called. I now remember where I heard it before the war. It was at Queen's Hall a couple of years ago. After a new piece by Arnold Bax, two of your pieces were played. I thought your music delightful and memorable. It's so strange to meet you here under very different circumstances.'

'You're absolutely right, Target, but for heaven's sake don't let on to the others about it. They'd never leave me alone, asking for concert parties and compositions to celebrate the colonel's birthday or his relief from constipation. My life as a composer seems so long ago now. It's as if I've become a different person, in a way no longer capable of what I once did.'

'Of course I'll tell no one if that's what you wish. I can understand your feelings. Do you think that you'll go back to writing music when the war is finished?'

'Target, I must confess that I don't know. I'm sure my father would be happy if I were to take up a career in law. But I don't somehow think that will ever happen. Perhaps I'll be able to go back to composition and perhaps not. Will England be the same place anymore? I composed very little, a number of songs, *The Idylls* and a few other lesser pieces. Would the impetus to do more still be there?'

The two officers shook hands and went their separate ways. George knew that he could trust Target. He recognised that the younger man looked up to him and would never betray a confidence.

Towards the end of March George's brigade, the 68th, was taken over by Sir Henry Page-Croft, MP. He was the first territorial brigadier and was notoriously outspoken. His criticisms of certain senior officers had caused ripples, which had never troubled the Regular Army where things like that just weren't done. George liked the sound of Page-Croft. He approved of a risk-taker, a man who was not afraid of his own opinions, the sort of commanding officer who did not skulk in a chateau miles behind the front.

George found that, since the war began, he was tending to move to the political right. He did not consider himself a Tory. His father had always favoured the Liberal Party, with possible leanings from time to time in a more leftwards direction. George now tended to see things more in black and white than formerly. The war had to be won at all costs and George appreciated a brigadier who had given up his comfortable post as Member of Parliament for Christchurch to rough it on the front line as Sir Winston Churchill had been forced to do after Gallipoli. From what he heard, George judged that Churchill had proven to be an excellent officer who always put the safety and comfort of his men above his own.

One evening after a long march towards the front, George was writing a letter to his father. His soldier servant passed him a mug of tea and said to him: 'Sir, I hope you don't mind me asking. Do your letters home differ very much from ours?'

George looked at him keenly. It was obvious that the man had been turning the question over in his mind and wanted an answer.

'Sit down please. I have to read and censor many letters from privates and all ranks up to warrant officers. If there is a difference it's quite simple to tell. The letters that I read are mostly truthful and often contain bloody descriptions of battles and trench raids. Usually no punches are pulled and little attempt is made to lessen the horrors of war to those at home. Officers' letters seem to be mostly saying: "I am fine and in good spirits. The front is quiet and there is very little risk of casualties. Thank you for the pink socks granny knitted for me. Keep your pecker up on the home front."

We cannot always seem to tell the truth and only seem to complain about the weather or the mud. We don't say: "Corporal X's head was blown off the other night. He was standing next to me and staggered about for a minute before collapsing and soaking my boots with blood." We tend to say: "There was a spot of bother the other night. We lost Corporal X. He died instantly and did not suffer at all. We shall miss him." Do you see what I mean? We are not always as truthful as you are. My stepmother is of a very nervous disposition and could not bear to read about things as they really are. Even so, I'm sure that her imagination works overtime when she thinks of me in the trenches.'

'Thank you, sir. I think that the ordinary soldier is more used to seeing life as it is. It's good to tell the family back home what we are going through so that they can share our lives out here. I hope you won't take offence at my question, sir.'

'Certainly not. Frankness should be at the heart of how every man deals with his fellows. I collect old folk songs from different parts of England. Many of them, though pretty and charming on the surface, are about death, the betrayal of love and things like that. They're not pleasant but they're real. People want the truth, even if we sometimes tend to understate it to spare the feelings of gentlefolk.'

'I always used to think that officers never swore or blasphemed, sir. Since I've been out here I see how we are all very much the same. I very much like serving an officer who I can sometimes talk to and learn from. Thank you, sir.'

George did not quite know what to say so he gave the man his dusty boots to clean before turning in for the night. He felt his responsibility most keenly as an officer that night. He hoped that Brigadier Page-Croft would be approachable when the time came that he needed his advice.

By April 1916 the first conscripts were due to begin basic training in England and eventually trickle into depleted regiments. George felt a little sorry for these men; they would be given little choice as to which regiment they would be sent to. Many would not be of the same quality as the earlier volunteers; some would have to be shown how to fight and to survive. Most would be fine. The transition from civilian to soldier would inevitably be harder for these new men than for those who had gone before.

Many things indicated to George that a major Allied offensive would take place in the summer. Pressure had to be taken off the French fighting valiantly to the south. Verdun was turning rapidly into stalemate once again, with no French breakthrough to the flat expanse of ground leading into Germany.

George put his money on a 'big push' somewhere on the chalk downs well south of Belgium. Perhaps the region around the Somme and Ancre rivers would become the place where the Allied armies could push the kaiser's armies back across the border to Germany.

Many gallant soldiers had arrived from Canada and South Africa, ready to fight for the Empire to which they were still tied. They were all volunteers and were pretty tough. A number came from rural areas, where harsh conditions gave them physical fitness and a resolute character.

George had to admit that he had had a fairly easy war so far. In a letter home he wrote: 'It is difficult to realise that we have really come through a winter campaign; I suppose one can consider it satisfactory as a test of physical fitness, though we certainly have been lucky, the worst weather nearly always having found us in billets. We have been equally fortunate as regards the attentions of the enemy, and there must be few battalions with seven months' trench experience whose total killed amount to less than fifty.'

As April gave way to May the beautiful spring weather continued to grace the blighted landscape. George's battalion went back once again to the trenches, winding their way for hundreds of yards along damaged communication trenches, past dead men in all stages of decay, through shell-shattered woods that now resembled discarded chewed toothpicks, through rusty barbed wire and the debris of a long war of attrition. Concentration must be maintained at all costs. George had seen too many men die from a brief lapse of attention.

The tedium of it all was getting to everyone. The moaning, whistling and howling of shells was as alarming as the sudden explosions and constant dangers of snipers and bombs. One learned to distinguish between the different types of shells and to name them. Instinctively one often knew which were dangerous and which would fall short or over-shoot the trench.

The men had to be kept busy. Rifle and kit inspections were constant and were vital to the maintenance of fighting effectiveness. Personal hygiene came a close second, with foot inspections at regular intervals and insistence on every man being clean shaven except for the usual moustache, which remained a matter of choice. George was amazed at how good the men's morale was. It was obvious that major fighting was taking place nearby. The chance of the battalion being sent in was a constant source of enthusiasm and dread in equal measure.

The news that filtered southwards to the 13th Durhams was not encouraging. To George it left only one probability, that of a major offensive in the upland region of the Somme. Once again the Germans would have the advantage; their trenches were mainly on comparatively high ground, up to 150 metres above sea level. But once the high ground was taken the Allied armies would descend to the Flanders plain with an impetus that would sweep all before it. But how could the German trenches be softened up to the point that a coordinated infantry attack could over-run them?

While pondering this weighty question George went home on leave at the end of May. He was in fine spirits. He spent a lot of time at his father's house in Hampstead. His stepmother seemed in better health; married life was obviously suiting her. Sir Alex was full of plans and he took George on a number of walks with the dogs on Hampstead Heath. With London spread at their feet the conflict seemed a long way away. At the back of George's mind was the forthcoming attack, which he hoped would turn the whole course of the war in the Allies' favour.

He went to a number of shows and saw some old friends. He regretted not being able to pop in on Ralph Vaughan Williams, who was still away driving ambulances somewhere in France. He would have liked to have talked once more about music and the future, but it was not to be.

It took over two days to travel from London back to his post. George spent a comfortable night in Boulogne, a town he had come to like. The few days in the trenches was full of the usual incidents: snipers, wiring parties, the usual 'hates', reconnaissance patrols and foul weather, which made the chore of completing endless paperwork doubly damp and frustrating. An alarming number of senior officers were sent home 'sick'. Most of the soldiers knew that they had 'cracked up' due to long exposure to enemy fire and the threat of attack. George and his fellow junior officers were more resilient and more in touch with the men whom they commanded.

There now was a feeling of change in the air. George felt that it was a tension that some of the Germans could well have picked up. The incidences of random firing increased, as did the artillery bombardments. George wondered how many of the men of his battalion would survive the coming battle.

The month of June alternated fine, sunny weather with days of rain that flooded the trenches and made everything twice as miserable. The chalk of the Somme turned greasy and slippery and it proved hard to get out of wet clothes. One damp evening George was sharing a dugout with Lieutenant Target. Apart from the distant crump of the occasional shell it was all quiet as the occasional drip fell from the ceiling. The dugout smelled of damp, of feet and of stale tobacco. The two officers were writing up reports, kit lists and conduct sheets. George looked up to find

Target staring at him.

'George, old man, I've been thinking about this religion business. I've always taken it for granted, given that my old man's quite religious. What worries me is the question of how a loving God can allow such a foul situation as this war. Why can't He just bloody well stop it. He'd convert thousands of people and everyone would be happy.'

'We can always hope for a miracle,' George replied, 'but I don't set much store by the possibility of one happening. If God exists, and I think He might, He didn't create us as slaves but as free men. If we were slaves we could be controlled for better or worse. As free men we make our own mistakes and find our own solutions.'

'So did God create us and set us loose with no instructions to the doom of an unspeakable war?'

'I think you'll find that the instructions are there if we look for them. But other things like greed and the lust for power get in the way. This is not the way that God wants us to live. He must be really cheesed off with us.'

'An interesting thought, George. If we are sad about this war then God must be beside Himself with grief.'

'I think so too. The Germans have chaplains and church services just as we do. They love music and the good things of life. So why are we fighting them?'

'Because we've been ordered to do so and they've been ordered to fight us. God didn't order men to kill each other.' Target sighed. 'He didn't send us these bloody forms to fill in either! Let's get our heads down and finish them up before we turn in.'

'Quite right Noel. Even God doesn't know when the forms and the war are going to end. How can He? Let's leave it there.'

'Before we do … George, why did we join the Army? I think I know why I did. It all sounds a bit unreal and vague now. I wanted to do my bit for the country I grew up in and love. That sounds trite but it's now even more true than when I started. What about you?'

'Well, Noel, it's all those things and one more in my case. The war gave me something to do. …'

Chapter Eight

The Somme

As one of the older and more experienced subalterns, George was becoming increasingly aware of the bigger picture; his mind was turning from tactics to strategy. From various hints from senior officers and other sources, he confirmed his view that the Allied attack would take place around the River Ancre, mainly north of the River Somme. He examined maps and pre-war guides to the Département of the Somme and worked out how he would attack the Germans.

The Roman road from Albert in the west to Bapaume in the east was about thirteen kilometres long and as straight as a die. It rose gradually from near the River Ancre on the outskirts of Albert on to chalk downs, fertile arable land with no hedges and numerous small woods and clumps of trees. There was a village every two or three kilometres and brick farms every few hundred metres. The names of the villages – La Boisselle, Pozières, Contalmaison and Martinpuich – would become very familiar to him in the next few weeks.

This gently rising and undulating chalk dome of land had changed beyond all recognition. Whole trench systems zigzagged across the now bare hills: two sets of three main trenches facing each other, the Allied trenches generally on the lower ground to the west, the German trenches on the tops of the hills. Each system consisted of a forward trench, a support trench and a reserve trench. Communications trenches ran in all directions between and at right angles to the main trenches, and saps, short exploratory trenches, were thrown out a little way towards the enemy trenches.

The Allied trenches were not designed to be inhabited for long. The idea of a moving war had not been entirely abandoned by High Command, who still hoped for decisive cavalry charges to clear the field. Trenches were intended as temporary accommodation and as stepping-off points.

The German trenches were generally much more substantial, with deep and comfortable dugouts, sometimes made cheerful by floral wallpaper. They were better supplied from a not too distant Fatherland. At the beginning of the war, rations were better: fresh meat and vegetables, wine and coffee. By 1916, however, the Fatherland was gradually becoming exhausted and the view from the top of the hill was not bringing Paris any nearer.

Field Marshal Haig had cautiously approved the big push forward on the Somme. He continued to have his doubts and was unhappy when the French Army moved to the south. This left the British Army – eventually to be supported by the Australian, New Zealand, Canadian and South African armies and small detachments of soldiers from the West Indies and other colonies – to attack uphill on a roughly twelve-mile front.

A huge bombardment of the German trenches was planned. Every available piece of artillery was pressed into service. The bombardment began on 23 June and continued unrelentingly for a solid week of mostly bad weather. British spotter planes had photographed every section of the German trench network and the guns were laid to smash every defence dug by the Hun. Any soldier subjected to prolonged enemy artillery fire involuntarily evacuates his bowels at some point. Others go mad in the enclosed trenches and dugouts. It becomes an intolerable strain on everyone.

The intense bombardment by a million and a half shells could be seen from miles away, illuminating the underside of the louring rain clouds. Faint percussions could be detected in London, a constant distant throb that alerted those in the know that the big push was about to begin. After the bombardment George was sent north from Millencourt with his brigade to Albert. They spent the first night in trenches not far from the Roman road to Bapaume. Looking up the gentle downland slope

George could see no trees or buildings. Where there had been a wood, only a few splintered sticks remained standing. All crops had been blasted, trampled and destroyed.

Turning round and looking over the parados, on 3 July, George saw what was left of the town of Albert. Many houses were roofless shells with rubble spilling into the streets. Above the dome of the basilica the gilded statue of the Virgin Mary holding out the Christ child hung out at a drooping and precarious angle.

'It looks to me as if she is about to throw the baby down into the street,' remarked Target, who was on his way to inspect his platoon's rifles.

'They also say that when the Virgin falls to the ground the war will be over,' George replied.

'Perhaps it depends on which side knocks her down,' was Target's parting shot from over his shoulder as he passed along the trench.

Two days earlier, on 1 July, the weather had finally cleared and, while George and the brigade were still at Millencourt the attack began at seven-thirty in the morning. Rum was issued from the big SRD jars, weapons and kit once more checked and whistles were blown to signal the beginning of the assault. Men clambered anxiously up short wooden ladders and jumped over the parapet laden with half their weight in kit. Despite their racing hearts, dry mouths and shaking limbs, most men were confident that a week's heavy bombardment by the big guns had all but destroyed the enemy lines, as well as most of the enemy. The order had been given to march, not run, up the slope with rifles slung. The men spread out so as not to bunch up. They walked uphill with their heads up, expecting only sporadic resistance, a few spatters of rifle fire, the odd 'potato masher' grenade.

Within a very few minutes, under a clear blue sky made carefree by the shrill song of larks in many parts of the fourteen-mile front, the whole situation changed. The German Maxim gunners emerged from their deep concrete bunkers, their fields of fire already carefully calculated, set up their belt-fed machine guns, and started to fire deliberate bursts into the mass of men surging up the hills towards them.

Whole swathes of men fell in rows while more took their places. The dead and wounded lay in neat ranks while their mates stepped over them to be mowed down in their turn. In a quarter of an hour the number of British casualties was equal to the whole population of the Somerset county town of Taunton. By the end of that first day 19,240 British soldiers lay dead on the lower slopes of the chalk downland, killed by machine-gun, rifle and artillery fire. 'It was,' wrote Siegfried Sassoon, who was there, 'a sunlit version of hell.'

The total British casualties of 1 July, the first day of the Battle of the Somme, were nearly 60,000 men. Some ground was gained, but most of the fighting ended in stalemate on that day, the Allied forces no closer to their prey. Ground that should have been taken in hours was to take weeks or months to wrest from a determined and well-trained enemy. It was the worst day in the history of the British Army.

On 3 July George and Noel Target were preparing to help lead their company out of the trench. They had little idea of what they would find. George would make no mention of the field first-aid posts with their rows of dead covered in bloody blankets, waiting to be buried. Here a booted foot stuck out at an angle, there a grimy clenched hand hung from a stretcher. Wounded men were everywhere: lying on filthy stretchers waiting to be treated, hobbling back to the rear with their eyes fixed on the ground in front of them, or being carried on stretchers by exhausted men with red crosses on their arms.

Dumps of ammunition and supplies were stacked under tarpaulins away from the first-aid posts. Dead artillery and transport horses pros-trate in groups slowly turned their hooves to the sky as they bloated and rolled. Their yellow teeth were bared as if in pain or surprise.

George had remarked earlier that, although they could see the muzzle flashes of the artillery, they heard little of the percussion. It seemed that most of the sound passed over them, to be heard more acutely several miles behind the line. A strange calm engulfed the tense, watchful men as they followed their officers up a gentle rise far to the right of the Albert to Bapaume road.

George was in charge of the bombing party. He was confident that the Mills bombs with their short fuses would be effective at fairly short

range. Festooned with bombs in haversacks and a number in his pockets
he felt like a Christmas tree. The bombs were like eggs, sturdy up to a
point. He tried not to slip or trip on what lay underfoot. A lark trilled
overhead and he thought of his friend Ralph driving an ambulance somewhere along the front. He sincerely hoped that he would not need his
services that day.

He led a select group of men, small, wiry and often profane bombers.
Their sense of humour was infectious and they were utterly ruthless. Many
had played village cricket in County Durham and knew how to throw
and how to keep a clear head. They could be relied on to concentrate on
the job in hand and not to hesitate when a target presented itself. Each
man was festooned like George but also carried a rifle with fixed bayonet;
George carried his pistol cocked in one hand and a trench map in the
other. He counted the paces and, as the ground rose before him, had a
good idea of where the German trenches were. They were heading for
Bécourt Wood. They did not know what they would find in the wood's
ruins. Would it be a starting-off point for an attack or a reserve position?
Would it be proper action at last or another instance of 'hurry up and wait'?

George knew that the Glosters were fighting on the other side of the
Albert to Bapaume road. He wondered if Ivor was among them. He felt
that a man of such a highly strung disposition should not be slogging
uphill into enemy fire. But perhaps Ivor, like himself, could profit from
the imposition of order and discipline in his life. Perhaps the war had
'given him something to do'.

The company reached the remains of Bécourt Wood without much
trouble after following a railway embankment around the southern outskirts of Albert. The odd spent bullet zipped overhead and artillery fire
seemed to come from three directions. The wood had formerly
surrounded a crossroads and slotted inbetween the villages of Bécourt
and Contalmaison further up the slope. Contalmaison was still most
definitely in German hands. From the wood 500 yards to the north-west
it appeared to be a ruined chateau with piles of bricks and shattered timber.

What had been Bécourt Wood was now an artillery dump and a
cemetery of white plank crosses at tilted angles, some holed by bullets.
Some of the graves had piles of flints arranged round their bases, some

consisted of a cross that had fallen over. A few rusting rifles and helmets decorated the hastily dug graves. The majority appeared to be from Scottish or north-eastern regiments and were dated from before the Somme offensive.

George arranged for the men to bivouac as far from the ammunition dump as possible. A few of the men complained humorously about their salubrious billets.

'It isn't the dead you need to worry about but the live munitions,' remarked the company sergeant major. 'Kit inspection in ten minutes.'

The men were getting used to the occasional stray bullets and the crash of nearby ordnance. They seemed quite at home close to the front lines and ready for a fight. But they also knew that waiting was inevitable and so made the best of their enforced idleness. Sentries were posted and an all-round defensive position adopted in shallow trenches. Because of the nearness to the German lines nobody was quite sure where a possible enemy attack would come from.

As he peered over the low parapet in the direction from which the enemy might be expected to advance, George reflected on what he had said to Noel Target. It was true up to a point that the war had given him something to do. Becoming an Army officer had imposed an order and a discipline on his life that had been somewhat lacking in the days of peace. He remembered how happy he had been during the month-long festival of folk songs and dancing at Stratford-upon-Avon. He was occupied and felt that he was achieving quite a lot. He didn't have time to brood or worry about his compositions and how he was to earn a living. Life in the Army was similar: learning new skills, developing leadership and playing a part in the struggle to win the war.

But here on the Somme the enormous futility of it all was beginning to bear down on him. He had to fight the feeling of helplessness. He would turn it to his advantage when the fighting finally began; it would evaporate when he knew just what it was that he had to do. The waiting was tedious but had to be borne philosophically, without cynicism, trusting that the senior officers had got it right. In any case, he had the example of the men to live up to. They were tough and cheerful. Their lives in Civvy Street had not been easy and the pride they took in their work was transferred to their life in the Army. He would never let them down. They were what he was there for. They were the embodiment of the England that had generated the songs and dances that he so loved. These were the ordinary people of England, the people who really mattered, the backbone of a land made top heavy by rich lawyers and bankers. Although George was conservative in his politics he was beginning to feel that a change to the left was on the cards.

The warm sun beat down on his new steel helmet. It made him think of a shallow bowler, heavy and rather awkward. It would certainly protect the head from debris coming from above but a bullet fired straight at it would penetrate it easily. The strap was an annoyance. It was supposed to be worn on the chin rather than under it. The idea was that it then couldn't be grabbed from behind and twisted, saving the man from being throttled. But the strap over the chin compressed the lips and made sensible talking difficult.

George determined to get hold of a piece of sacking, rub it in the earth, and tie it over his helmet, blurring the shape and making him harder to spot. He never knew when his life could be saved by the helmet. The new German helmets were much more impressive, covering more of the side of the face and the neck. They were known as 'coal scuttles' by the British Tommies, who could always be relied upon to find a name for anything. He hadn't seen one; they had been issued at Verdun but not every German regiment possessed them yet. George had seen the distinctive boiled leather pickelhaube when he had glimpsed for a second figures in field grey. With spike removed and a canvas cover they would be effective against the slash of a sabre but not very effective against bullet or shrapnel.

'Enough musing on headgear,' George thought and, in a rare moment of quiet, thought about the fields and trees behind him, untouched by war. Just ahead was desolation: featureless land ploughed up by high explosives and sown with barbed wire, littered with corpses and equipment – an abomination of desolation. Yet beyond the extensive and tangled German lines was green countryside, streams, quiet woods and fields. 'This is what we are fighting for,' George fiercely mused.

Chapter Nine

Bailiff Wood: 7 July 1916

On 7 July a British attack was made on Bailiff Wood, which was sited over a kilometre away on a slight rise above Bécourt Wood. It had been a wood of saplings before the German artillery bombardment and was a step closer to the second set of German trenches which were just above the 150-metre contour above sea level, close to the summit of the downs; 10 metres higher, at 160 metres, was the windmill just beyond Pozières, the highest point on the battlefield and an important German observation point.

Pozières and Martinpuich were two small agricultural villages lying on each side of the gentle crest of the hills. Both had been reduced to dust and rubble by artillery. Pozières straddled the Albert to Bapaume road, Martinpuich a few hundred yards to the right of the road. If the second set of German trenches could be captured, the two villages would prove to be a hinge to moving northwards towards Mouquet Farm and Thiepval. When Thiepval was taken, strong German fortifications overlooking Beaumont Hamel would be overrun and the central part of the Somme battle would be virtually over.

In fact Pozières, only two kilometres from the first German line at La Boisselle, was supposed to have been taken on the first day of the battle, 1 July. In fact virtually no ground had been gained and over five weeks later the 13th Battalion of the Durham Light Infantry were ready to play their part in helping to gain a foothold towards Pozières. One problem was the village and chateau of Contalmaison, 400 yards to the south-east of Bailiff Wood. Enfilading artillery and machine-gun fire poured from the remains of the village. To take the wood would not be an easy task.

Just south of Bailiff Wood was the German reserve trench, the third back in the first set of German trenches. A few hundred yards to the north and dipping down to the east in front of Contalmaison was the first, or fighting trench, of the second set of German trenches. Behind them and uphill were the strongly held supply and reserve trenches known as the OG (Ost Graben) 1 and OG 2 lines. These trenches defended Pozières; an outlier known as Pozières Trench looped round the south of the village connecting to OG 1, the front fighting trench.

George and Noel set out from Bécourt Wood with their company commander and all the rest of the company to relieve the 12th Battalion DLI. They walked over the remains of the British trenches from which the Scottish and Tyneside regiments had attacked on 1 July. Enemy artillery fire was sporadic and not markedly dangerous. Advancing up Sausage Valley they began to see discarded equipment and groups of corpses lying where enemy fire had mown them down. One of the men remarked that he hadn't realised that so many of the Tyneside Scots were black men.

'Don't look at the faces,' growled a sergeant. 'They're starting to decompose, God rest their souls.'

Off to the left, near the ruins of the village of La Boisselle, the chalky lips of a huge crater could be seen, a strange sight in a featureless landscape.

'Lochnagar Crater blown by a mine on 1 July,' remarked Noel. The men stepped over bloating bodies and pieces of men. George had wondered if kilted soldiers really did not wear underpants, now he knew for sure that they did not. There was absolutely no dignity in war; hundreds of bodies left out in the sun and rain to rot emphasised further the inhumanity of it all.

Bullets began to zip and whine from in front of the company and from the right-hand flank. Although well spaced out, men began to fall, wounded, among their dead comrades. A machine gun opened up from the direction of Contalmaison. The captain calmly ordered the men to lie down in the nearest trench and take whatever small amount of cover they could find. Everyone began to dig into the coarse chalk, using entrenching tools and bayonets. Soon some better cover was available and the number of men hit decreased. A few walking wounded were sent to the rear.

'Crawling wounded more like,' remarked the company sergeant major, shaking a bandaged fist at the enemy.

Men fired aimed shots at the German trench. The Lewis gun was set up so that it could swivel from east to north in a defensive position. Soon the artillery barrage began. The German guns had difficulty finding their range in the featureless terrain. Most of the shells exploded behind the new trench, a few fell short and dangerously near the Durhams.

'Prepare for an enemy attack,' called Captain White. Men checked their ammunition and their bombs. Each chose a field of fire that interlocked with the men to his left and right. The guns roared and shells passed over with a noise like an express train. After a few minutes the barrage stopped. Men strained their eyes in the smoke and dust. Soon the bobbing heads of the attacking Germans appeared on the horizon. Several German machine guns started firing short bursts, unhurried staccato that mostly raised angry plumes of dust in front of the new trench.

'Hold your fire until they are in range,' shouted the captain.

George could see how the element of surprise was vital. When the bobbing heads became chest and arms holding glinting bayonets the captain gave the order to fire. 'Fire at Wilhelm,' he yelled.

'I think he means "Fire at will." He hasn't been quite himself of late,' Noel remarked coolly.

The Lewis gun began to sweep the ground to the east. The men kept up a rapid fire and Germans began to fall. Some threw up their arms before toppling over, some just collapsed in a heap. The noise of firing was too great to hear anything else; each man's death struggle was acted out in silence.

A few of the Durhams were hit and pitched forward or were pulled down to the bottom of the shallow trench. George had fired his rifle but had thrown no bombs. He had seen a few men fall but was not always sure if he had hit them or not. The Germans advanced no closer. They could be seen withdrawing in an orderly manner, leaving their dead and wounded to litter the ground between the Durhams and the ruins of Contalmaison. They would be back without a doubt, George thought.

The captain ordered the trench evacuated and a trench nearby enlarged and improved. Sentries were posted and a roll call was taken and first aid given to wounded men wherever possible. Amazingly no one had been killed, although a few men had sustained serious wounds. The dead of 1 July had to stay where they were, out in no man's land, until more ground was taken. It was going to be a hard slog.

Chapter Ten

Bailiff Wood: 8 July 1916

Next day, 8 July, the attack on Bailiff Wood began in earnest. Following a creeping barrage, the men of the 12th and 13th Battalions advanced towards the German trenches. Despite enfilade fire from their right flank they gradually gained ground. Some of the German wire had been broken and cast aside by the artillery bombardment and some had to be cut. It required strong wrists to cut the thick single strands of the German wire; this was no problem to the men who survived being shelled or shot at the wire.

George and his bombers advanced to the German lines, flinging fizzing grenades on to the men huddled there in defence. The shattering roar of the bombs could be heard but not the shrieks and groans of the mutilated men in the trench. George felt filthy and his throat dry as he ran around bodies, shell holes and wire. He directed his men to throw their bombs to the greatest effect. He felt the exhilaration of an obscene game of cricket whose aim was not to make runs but to kill as many of the opposition as possible. His uniform was torn and bloody and his hands bleeding from hastily handling lengths of tangled wire. His fine boots were scuffed and badly scratched and his slung rifle banged constantly at his shoulder.

Men fell on either side of him and lay still or scrambled blindly for cover. Bullets zipped and whined all round him. He scarcely noticed them, only being knocked sideways when a shell exploded almost soundlessly nearby. Skipping nimbly around half-noticed obstacles George and his bombing party reached a trench to see field grey figures retreating towards Contalmaison on the right flank. Bundles of grey shapes were strewn over the bumpy ground – a face or hand visible here, a booted foot there. There were no prisoners; only the motionless dead and severely wounded.

'Make sure they're dead,' George heard himself shouting. He drew his pistol preparing himself to shoot any man on the ground who would aim a weapon. Shots rang out all round him from the infantry who ran past him in pursuit of the retreating Germans. It appeared that the men on the ground, even those still in one piece, were too far gone to provide any further opposition. They had all done what they could.

George was startled to see a German sitting at ease at the bottom of the trench smiling pleasantly up at him. He showed no fear and seemed an amiable man. It was only the thin layer of dust on eyes glazed over that showed that he was dead. 'One less Alleyman,' George thought coldly as he stood panting, revolver in one hand, bomb in the other.

'Keep your head down if you please, sir,' came the calm voice of the RSM. George noticed that he kicked a Luger away from the outstretched fingers of a dead German infantry officer. The pistol slid down into the already littered German trench.

'No time for souvenirs,' George shouted to anyone who was in range to hear him.

A cold and rather damp night was spent in the former German trench. The dead enemy inhabitants were hoisted out and formed part of the new parapet facing the second system of German trenches that snaked round on two sides, protecting the villages of Pozières and Contalmaison. Enemy flares shot up into the dark sky all through the night and sporadic fire came from three directions. As drizzle enveloped the open fields George imagined Germans creeping towards him with rifle and bombs at the ready. He kept his nerve and was busy checking his men up and down the trench until first light, when everyone stood to in the grey dawn.

George nodded off in his filthy Burberry sitting on the fire step. Quite soon he was shaken awake by Target.

'George, it's the old man. There's something wrong. Come and see.'

Picking up his rifle and haversack of bombs George stumbled along the trench to a dugout that faced towards the enemy. It was deep and well constructed, with a gas cape hung over the entrance. George went down the steps to find the captain sitting at a rough table, hunched over and deadly pale with a sheen of sweat on his face.

'Hello sir, are you feeling all right?' George quietly asked.

The captain looked at him absently as if for the first time. 'Ah, George,' he said. 'Good man …' and collapsed slowly on to the earth floor. A stain had spread from under his left arm. George loosened his tunic, relieved that the stain was mostly dried blood. The captain groaned. 'Shell fragment,' he said. 'I'm so sorry. Take charge George.'

'Noel, please have two men take the CO to the rear on a stretcher as soon as it is safe to do so. Direct them along the communication trench back down towards Bécourt Wood. Send a runner ahead to alert the first-aid post. Get volunteers.'

'Certainly George. The CO's pulse seems strong even though he has lost consciousness. I'll make sure he's on his way back.'

It had been a very busy and confused day. George remembered a shell landing quite close to the trench and about a dozen officers and men being blown over by the explosion. George may even have lost consciousness for a moment. When he came to, with ringing ears, he was aware of movement all round him. He saw the CO being supported on his way back to the dugout. The captain had seemed shaken but unhurt further.

Three of the men had been killed that day, all from artillery fire. Privates Dale, Green and Hollingshead had been seen engulfed by shell fire. Nobody was sure if the bombardment had been British or German. George had no obvious ill effects except for a hearing loss in one ear. He very much hoped that this would prove a temporary handicap.

He realised with a quiet dawning of consciousness that he was now in charge of the company. He found the CSM and gave his orders before ordering a weapon inspection all along the trench. The men would soon know who was now in charge of them.

Chapter Eleven

Bailiff Wood: 9 July 1916

During the long, busy night George planned how the company would help to capture and secure the rest of Bailiff Wood. He was red-eyed and tired but felt alert and decisive nonetheless. With the help of Lieutenants Target and Clark and the senior NCOs he outlined his plan. The trench was to be extended into the wood under cover of darkness and fighting patrols would silence a number of machine-gun positions to the east and north of the wood.

One of the most lethal machine-gun nests was a few hundred yards away on the edge of the ruined village of Contalmaison. There was wire and the remains of a light narrow-gauge railway between the trench and the ruined village and precious little cover. George's patrol would have to take advantage of artillery barrages directed at the village. They would treat the bombardment as a creeping barrage, advancing directly behind the exploding shells and hoping all the time that the barrage wasn't pulled back. He sent runners back to advise that all barrages must only advance forwards. Having no field telephones at this stage of the advance he also wanted to know when the barrages would take place.

In the meantime, the enemy machine guns sent accurate fire to the trench at intermittent intervals, often raining gouts of earth along the parapet just above the heads of the resting soldiers. The German artillery fire was getting more accurate. It was only a matter of time before the range was found.

George was shaving in the dugout when a runner brought him the message with the time of the barrage and its length and range. With only an hour to prepare for the raid George wiped the soap from his chin and called an Operations Group.

With all men in the trench on full alert under the command of Noel Target, George briefed his bombers and issued them with a good number of grenades. He arranged for covering rifle fire and detailed the Lewis gunners to move around the trench firing short bursts at the German trench in front of Contalmaison. A close eye would have to be kept on the enemy lines that continued north of the village before curving round further up the hill and snaking below Pozières. This was the fighting trench, OG 1, that formed the first line of defence in the second series of the German trench system.

The barrage was due to begin just as dawn was breaking at 04.30 hours. There would not be much sun because of the drizzly weather and the mist that covered most of the battlefield. As the light strengthened George found the men hollow-eyed but very determined. When the barrage began Lieutenant Target would take a group of men and advance into the ruined wood to some trenches slightly uphill from their present position. They would take to these trenches and dig in, abandoning the present trench before the enemy artillery pounded it to oblivion.

George felt a faint warmth on his face and hands. From somewhere improbable birds were beginning to sing. He felt ready, committed, not at all afraid of what he was about to do. If he were to be killed then so be it. There would be no time for regrets, perhaps not even for pain. He lived now, for the moment, and for the success of what he was about to achieve. He checked his pistol and his bags of bombs. His batman would take charge of his rifle and keep it by his side. If there was time he would even clean it so that not a single speck of mud or dust could been seen down the barrel.

As George glanced at his watch the artillery barrage began. Shells fell only a couple of hundred yards in front of the trench where George's bombers waited. Then they started to fall further towards the German lines. 'Up and at 'em,' George shouted, waving his pistol towards the screaming shells and shattering blasts.

The bombing party rose as a man and scrambled up out of the trench, running at a crouch over scattered and trailing lengths of wire. Despite the barrage, the odd bullet zipped and whined past as the men advanced. A few men fell but the bombers, supported by riflemen on the flanks, ran on.

The slow clatter of the German Maxim gun revealed that it was positioned ahead and slightly to the left. George pointed his left hand towards it and the bombers moved uphill, taking advantage of any available cover: shell holes, shattered trees, the occasional ruined wall.

The barrage advanced over the battlefield, moving steadily eastwards. The ground exploded high into the air, the occasional clod or flint hitting George's helmet or the sleeve of his tunic. With bursting lungs and throats burning with the stink of cordite, the bombers came at last to the German fighting trench on the edge of the piles of rubble and splintered wood that was Contalmaison.

Not bothering to notice if there were many enemy in the trench; the bombers ran up to it and hurled their grenades straight down into it. The crack of rifle fire from both sides could hardly be heard as a series of sharp bangs marked the first grenades exploding in the trench. No shrieks or groans could be heard as the barrage progressed into the ruins of Contalmaison, blindly seeking out cellars and bunkers occupied by the enemy.

The German trench was empty in places, yet full of dead and dying field grey figures in others. George sent in the riflemen with bayonets fixed to sort out any wounded Germans who could still be dangerous.

The wretched machine gun still chattered to the left. George took a couple of bombers and the same number of riflemen and ran along the trench towards the flash of the gun. From a considerable distance he threw a grenade, which landed just behind the muzzle flash. There was a split second's silence in which he noticed that the barrage had finished, and then came a shattering roar. The gun stopped firing as a couple of figures rose briefly before falling flat behind the parapet. George ran on, lobbing more grenades at the gun. The intermittent rifle fire had stopped and finally George looked down on the smashed Maxim gun and its mangled crew lying at tortuous angles all around it. George felt glad that the gun was silenced but felt sad that the crew had met such a messy end. They had been very brave and had stayed at their post before being blasted and twisted into oblivion. He wished with all his heart that he didn't have to fight brave men.

That evening, in the relative quiet of the deepened trench the roll call was taken. The company had lost four men: Privates Ball, Carr, Noble and Walton. It could have been worse. The next day it certainly would be.

Chapter Twelve

Bailiff Wood and Contalmaison: 10 July 1916

At 08.15 hours on another overcast day, the attack on Contalmaison was launched. A Company, led by Lieutenant Butterworth acting as company CO, joined the men of other companies of the 13th and 12th Battalions, who scrambled out of their filthy trench to the shrill accompaniment of whistles to strike towards Contalmaison.

During the night George, reeling from tiredness and punch drunk, had checked the sentries for the eighth or ninth time. He could not sleep when he knew that brave men had been ordered to stand to while their officers slept. Noel Target and Lieutenant Clark were also keeping watch.

George found that one of the sentries, a young miner, was shaking uncontrollably. He put his hand on his shoulder. 'Are you afraid?' he asked.

'Yes sir,' replied the soldier.

'Do you think I'm not?' asked George.

'I don't know, sir.'

'Well I'm bloody terrified and it's a good thing I'm wearing khaki trousers. We're no different, you and I. I just can't afford to show it. We both have a job to do and we must support one another. We must try to do our best.'

'You're right, sir. You can depend on me just as I will depend on you, sir.'

'Well done man. You've made me feel better. I'll be counting on you tomorrow.'

'Thank you, sir. I'll do my best, you can count on it.'

With a quick pat on the man's back George moved on, thinking of the night before Agincourt when King Henry moved among his soldiers, unable to sleep and dreading the outcome of the morrow's fight. He certainly didn't feel a bit like King Harry.

In the end, the attack came as a form of relief. All nerves vanished in the advance. The enemy opposition was stiff and determined, but with the help of a creeping barrage, advances were made. George couldn't help but think of the barrage which, a couple of days ago, had forced them to retreat from Bailiff Wood. The relative ease of getting back to the wood had made him think that the barrage must have come from his own side. Communications were terrible; radio wires were constantly cut by shell fire and the bodies of numerous runners lay out in the open behind the trenches, cut down by shells and rifle fire. Pigeons were worse than useless. The Antwerp pigeons that were the mainstay of aerial communications were only interested in food and sex and were known as 'twerps', a term that became applicable to soldiers who refused to use their minds and lacked initiative.

George and his bombing party continued to do good work. They were getting used to seeing men torn open and grovelling in their own intestines begging to be shot and put out of their agony. Many men complied, not out of hate but from common humanity. George had no time to think. He barely noticed the shattering explosions and blasts that knocked him sideways or the bullets that whined past his head. He fought on in a calm, detached bubble, directing bombers and riflemen against a mainly hidden enemy. Every inch was hard fought and came at the cost of men's lives. There was no time for contemplation. Rage played no part in the fighting; cool, detached, heartless logic determined where the next bombs should go, where the Lewis gun should pour its leaden death.

During the afternoon George found himself in a strange trench near the piles of brick and stone that were once Contalmaison with its church and chateau. While men streamed towards the rubble George found himself ordered to withdraw his company to the rear while another company took their place. These fresh men were cleaner, less haggard, and lacked the dull, haunted look that every man in George's company had in his eyes. They were to finally take Contalmaison on 10 July.

It seemed hours later when the roll-call was taken. By then the weary men were back at Bécourt Wood in relative safety after a scramble back across wire, broken ground and corpses. George was so weary that some of the dead men seemed to speak to him. Their messages made little sense, consisting mainly of sibilant gibberish.

When the roll-call of A Company was taken, the men sat listlessly on the ground. Seven men would no longer be coming back to the rear, would no longer exchange smutty remarks, drink weak beer or piss into empty shell cases. The dead and missing were noted down: Private Alliston, Corporal Pulford, Lance Sergeant Purvis, Lance Corporal Scott, Private Strickland, Private Todd, Private Wearmouth. George felt responsible for all their deaths.

'Cheer up George,' said Target. 'We could have lost a whole lot more men and gained nothing, you know. We did well today, thanks to the men and to your leadership.'

George was speechless and could only nod. He slipped into a heavy sleep from which he was roused to make a report to a senior officer. In his semi-conscious state he half heard the words 'Military Cross' before passing out in his chair, to be dragged back to his tent by his attentive soldier servant.

Chapter Thirteen

Albert: 11 to 15 July 1916

Back at Albert the Virgin Mary still hung off the church steeple at an impossible angle, offering the baby Jesus to the vertiginous drop into the street below. But the British Army clung to its tenuous hold near Contalmaison. Reinforcements were on their way. The Australians were coming; large, tanned, rangy men used to the outdoors and used to thinking for themselves. They had distinguished themselves in Belgium, mining, digging and fighting in their own independent way.

The men of A Company all had the chance to have a bath at a brewery, where they exchanged their filthy and tattered uniforms for new ones with, for the immediate future, no lice in the seams. Hair and moustaches were cut. Thanks to his servant's skill with a needle George's uniform was mended. Tears and holes were expertly sewn up, frayed cuffs neatened, and his field service uniform made presentable. George's hair and bushy moustache were disciplined and he scrubbed himself raw. If only he could get the smell of cordite and death from his memory and nostrils.

A quantity of his favourite tobacco had arrived from Hampstead so he stoked up his best pipe and puffed contentedly away. The battlefield horrors faded a little as he inspected the men and saw to their welfare. He told them how well they had done and how pleased he was with them. He knew that he would always be able to rely on them and that thought made him proud. The men were what he was fighting for. He looked forward one day to returning them safe to their native shore, to sending them back to the cottages, mines, forges and workshops in the north-east of England. He hoped that most of them would survive the coming battle.

After Contalmaison the push was on to capture Pozières at the top of the chalk downs. Then the aim would be to strike north towards the strongpoint of Mouquet Farm and finally Thiepval, where the German redoubts menaced further progress up the deep valley of the Ancre. With help from the Australians, Canadians, and South Africans, the British Army could achieve victory at last on the Somme before striking east into the Flanders plain and chasing the Hun back to Berlin.

George sat cleaning and oiling his battered pistol. It was a rare moment of quiet when he didn't have to think about his men.

'George, I've been thinking about what we'll do with ourselves if we survive this war. What will you do?

'A good question Noel. I feel so far removed from music and composition that I wonder how I can ever get back to it. But I can't imagine doing anything else. That's what the war's done to me. It's possible that I will never have it in me to compose another piece of music again. On the other hand it might all come back. Impossible to say. What about you?'

'The Colonial Service I suppose. Some beastly hot place in India or Africa. I can't help feeling, however, that the Empire is on the slide. The world will be very different when the kaiser's out of the equation. We might be the men who are left behind.'

George wondered if the England of village greens, cricket, pubs, and morris dancing would ever change and realised, with a jolt, that it could. The war altered many things. War memorials would spring up everywhere, not just the few that originated from the South African War. There would be few towns and villages spared. The land would be bereft and sad; life would become like an A.E. Housman poem, full of regret for times and men past. The blue remembered hills would not be in France and Belgium but in the heart of England, where, according to Housman, they had always been. How many musicians, folk singers and morris dancers had already quietly died over here?

The nagging question came back. Would he ever again be able to take up his composition? Had his vision and his sensibilities already been shattered? Who was he? Was he the struggling composer who was just beginning to make his way in the world of British music and dancing? Or was he a man of decisive action, a leader of men who was capable of incredible violence? Could these two sides be reconciled and could a post-war synthesis ever be reached?

George found himself thinking, once again, of Shakespeare, who must have understood the dichotomy of intellect and action: 'There is nothing either good or bad, but thinking makes it so.'

'A penny for your thoughts, George,' said Noel Target, appearing suddenly over George's left shoulder.

'Not much going on in the brain department at the moment,' George replied.

'Same here, old man. It's action that will be needed but also the sense to get it right. We can fight our way to the top of the hill if we try hard enough and go about it carefully. It's really up to us now, not the generals or the staff officers.'

'You're right, Noel. We've been here for long enough. Let's get it done. We can think about it later, analyse our moves and plans when the appropriate time comes if we are still around. But now is the time for action, pure and simple. Action based on sound sense, simple as that.'

On 18 July the whole tactical equation changed with the entry of the Australians into the battle. They were 1 Anzac Corps, under the command of Lieutenant General Sir William Birdwood. The Australian 1st and 2nd Divisions were pressed into action before their staff had been properly set up, because of the haste of General Hubert Gough to take Pozières. The commanding officer of 1 Anzac Division, Brigadier General Sir H.B. Walker, was unhappy with this decision but nevertheless pushed on, deploying his division south of Pozières.

On 23 July, after a couple of postponements and a very heavy artillery barrage that reduced any semblance of housing in Pozières to rubble and dust, the attack was mounted. On the left flank, north of the Albert to Bapaume road, was the 48th Division of the British Army, comprising the 144th Brigade, 1/4th and 1/6th Gloucesters; and 145th Brigade, 1/5th Gloucesters and 1st and 4th Ox and Bucks Light Infantry; in the centre, south of Pozières was 1 Anzac; and on the right flank, south-east of Pozières were 1st and 3rd Corps of the British Army.

The Gloucesters and Ox and Bucks advanced under a creeping barrage on the left flank from a point north-east of Ovillers towards the northern extremity of Pozières where the shattered remains of the church and the cemetery were sited. Supported by machine-gun fire and Stokes mortars, infantry and bombing parties advanced towards the northern edge of the village. German troops were seen to retreat, carrying a machine gun but leaving the base behind on the ground. Enemy resistance stiffened and the Gloucesters, having taken some trenches, were forced to retire. The Ox and Bucks fared no better; having taken ground with much hand-to-hand fighting they were also forced to retire. Only D Company of the 1st (Bucks) Battalion gained ground because they attacked before the creeping barrage had lifted and surprised the enemy in their trench. B Company sustained such heavy casualties that they were also forced to retire.

Relieved by the Royal Berkshires, the gains of the day were generally held. In the centre the Australians were more successful, advancing through ruined orchards to take most of the village up to, and including, parts of OG 1, the front, or fighting trench of the second line of defence. The slaughter was terrible, but the Australians had also taken Pozières Trench, which encircled the south-west part of the village.

Some deep German dugouts had miraculously survived the intense bombardment of the previous few days. From one of them, later called 'Medical Bunker', emerged an officer in a long grey greatcoat with his hands held high. He was the commandant of Pozières, Hauptmann Ponsonby Lyons. His distinguished British surname was thanks to an English grandfather. He was marched away, presumably into captivity, by Captain Vowles, an Australian officer who hopefully spared his life. A number of the commandant's fellow officers were shot down rather than taken prisoner.

To the south-east of the village, the German Pozières Trench, now in Australian hands, crossed OG 1 and OG 2 trenches to become Munster Alley, which ran back to Switch Line, the third German trench in front of the village of Martinpuich, which ran back to the third German trench system. By the end of July, Munster Alley formed the boundary between the Australians in the centre and the British on the right flank.

Munster Alley, a German trench, was not named after the north German city where heretics were held in cages on the wall of the cathedral tower. It had been taken briefly, but not held, by the 2nd Battalion, Royal Munster Fusiliers, in an earlier unsuccessful action. Munster Alley was in the parish of Contalmaison, the ruined village that remained partially occupied by the enemy. It lay a couple of kilometres to the south west of Pozières in a fold of the downs, providing enfilade fire to troops attempting to infiltrate Munster Alley from below. Munster Alley was to play a large part in the life and fate of Lieutenant George Kaye Butterworth.

Chapter Fourteen

17 to 25 July 1916

General Rawlinson's policy of 'bite and hold' was being demonstrated by the Durhams in the fight for Pozières. Men went over the top with the clear aim and devout hope of finally taking the village. They advanced at a crouch with bayonets fixed and eyes on the rutted horizon. As they skirted round shell holes, filthy tarpaulins were lifted and German machine guns opened up from beneath their concealment. Bombers ran between holes blasting machine gunners. But they could not be everywhere. Many were mown down by small-arms fire and disappeared beneath shell fire that dropped on them from the German guns.

The biting did not get to the ruins of the centre of Pozières. The holding consisted of digging the front-line trench deeper and extending it by joining up fresh shell holes. George was everywhere, filthy and hoarse, exhorting men in their braces to dig harder and deeper, even reaching for a pick here, a shovel there, and digging in the filthy chalk to make the trench better and more effective. He pulled dead men aside to make room for the living as shells crashed and thundered down all round him. Mud and chalk flew in the air as he directed rifle fire towards the greatest concentration of the enemy. Bullets zipped overhead and machine-gun fire shredded sandbags all along the parapet. Men fell and slumped silently in the huge roar and shriek of battle. Even with their mouths wide open they could not be heard.

There was little to distinguish night from day. A thick drizzle had started to fall, the sheets of rain lazily soaking every man labouring in the trench. No man noticed the rain as George detailed some to dig, some to fire through narrow loopholes in the sandbags and others to take the wounded back through winding communications trenches to the first-aid posts. The occasional crash of German rifle grenades at points up or down the trench lit up the sky. Coloured flares drifted eerily down through the mist.

The centre of the village of Pozières remained in enemy hands, so near yet so far away. George, normally a soft-spoken clean-mouthed man, found himself inventing ever more fanciful and obscene phrases to inspire his men at their tasks. The look of momentary amusement on some men's faces told him that his invective was reaching them.

Eventually the Durhams were relieved. Surrounded by the slumped figures of dead and dying men who had given all they had, George, as if in a weary dream, saw large men in floppy hats coming along the trench on both sides of him.

'You're relieved. Bugger off down the communication trench and go back to Frenvillers. Look sharpish now!'

George gave a thumbs up to a young Australian officer who seemed to be boiling over for a fight. He put his mouth to his ear and briefed him as thoroughly as he could, leaving nothing out. Pieces of chalk and lumps of clay flew past his head as he collected his men to go to the rear. He made sure that the walking wounded had men to guide them and he asked for volunteers to act as stretcher-bearers. Men continued to fall all round him. Finally, he put Noel at the head of the column and brought up the rear himself. The able-bodied would have to go ahead, followed by the walking wounded and stretcher cases. George slid between the greasy chalk walls of the communication trench. He had never felt so weary in his life. His throat burned, his eyes were red, the stubble on his chin and cheeks itched. He could hardly place one muddy boot in front of the other. When he pulled his pipe out of his pocket he found that it was in three pieces. He had bitten through the stem before falling down and snapping what remained of it. He didn't now have the energy to fling it into no man's land but dropped it between his boots and trod it into the bottom of the trench.

Once clear of the communication trench the long march began. But first of all George wanted to see who was with him and in what shape were the remains of his company. New uniforms were now ragged and frayed, holes ripped by wire, cloth soaked in blood or a ghostly white streaked by chalk. Some men peered through filthy bandages wrapped round their heads. In one case it was only the position of the glowing tip of a Woodbine that showed where a man's head was situated.

George ordered a rest and collected water and rations to give out in equal measure to each man. After ten minutes he roused the men, most of whom were falling asleep and, with himself at the head, led the column back towards Albert.

They didn't arrive at Frenvillers until four o'clock in the morning. Some men were walking in their sleep, others were at the limit of their strength and endurance. Yet no man had fallen out. Encouraged by George's firm but gentle prodding they had all made it back to a place of respite.

Just over a week later, at the Orders Group at Frenvillers, thirteen miles behind the lines, George looked at his officers and senior NCOs. Noel Target was there and Lieutenant Clark, both looked rested and ready for what was about to come.

'Our aim now is to secure the high ground to the east of Pozières. Munster Alley bisects OG 1 and OG 2 trenches and is the demarcation between the Australians and us. We will be in constant danger from not only the enemy fire but also our own. There are no landmarks at all. Our aim is to take the ridge and the new Switch Line which is behind the village roughly parallel to OG 1 and OG 2. We are still liable to enfilade fire from the right flank. It will not be easy but we will succeed. It could take a long time with heavy losses. We have come so far and we cannot turn back. We are fully committed now and, with God's help and with the splendid work by the Australians, we shall take the Switch Line and the windmill and turn to the north towards Thiepval. Thank you gentlemen. Are there any questions?'

'Mr Butterworth.'

'Company Sergeant Major.'

'What we are about to take from the enemy should have been ours over three weeks ago, on the first day of the battle. Why is it all taking so long?'

'It's true that we should have taken Pozières and the second German trench system on 1 July. The Germans were much better prepared than we thought and now, through persistence and the great fighting quality of our troops, we will take it. Bite and hold. Adversity breeds character and, make no bones about, we will win!'

'Very good, sir. We'll be with you every inch of the way. And we'll make plenty of bones!'

Chapter Fifteen

26 July 1916

Lieutenant George Sainton Kaye Butterworth, now unofficially acting captain, found himself, with his A Company, in Black Watch Alley between Bailiff Wood and Contalmaison. The forward trench had been excavated in a valley roughly parallel to the straight Albert to Bapaume road, which was concealed behind a ridge to the north.

Pozières was still in enemy hands despite being reduced to a mound of pink brick fragments. The Germans in the Switch Line presented a great problem for George and his men. Not only were the Durhams liable to be attacked from the ridge near Pozières but they would come under fire from the side from the enemy positions to the south.

As usual George ordered his men to reinforce the trench. They dug steadily into the dusk, reinforcing the parapets and deepening the trench. From time to time German shells came over, probing the position, collapsing it in places and burying men who had to be frantically gouged out of the earth. That night there were several cases of shell shock, particularly among the men who had been buried. Tired nerves were shredded and George had every sympathy for the shattered men. It didn't make his task easier; George constantly reassured exhausted men and bolstered them.

The time in Black Watch Alley was limited. It was a rest stop on the march up on to the ridge. The battalion was to occupy Munster Alley on the dome of the downlands of the Somme. From there they would begin to fight their way northwards along the ridge towards the strong-points of the windmill and Mouquet Farm. The whole axis of the battle was beginning to turn.

Before preparing to leave the entrenched position to march uphill behind a barrage, Noel Target stumped along the trench festooned by the rifles of the men sent back down the hill.

'Sometimes I wonder if we'll ever get clear of the parish of Contalmaison,' he grumbled. 'It's one step forward and two back. I just hope they keep us at it long enough to get to the top of the ridge and see the view.'

'According to my map,' said George, 'the parish of Martinpuich, just over the crest of the ridge, is in the departement of Pas de Calais and into Artois. So it will be goodbye Contalmaison, farewell Picardie.'

'Shall we sing 'It's a long way to Tipperary' or 'On the Crest of a Wave'?'

'Let's just get there and then decide!'

'Righty-ho George. We live in hope.'

The march up to Pozières was easier than previously anticipated. With Contalmaison in Allied hands the enfilading fire came from farther away. With the various simultaneous attacks on the copses and woods south of Pozières the enemy had its attention diverted from trying to kill the Durhams. The battalion moved across the usual devastated landscape, emerged from the shallow valley and on to the edge of the ridge. With the booming of artillery not far away and the vicious whine of the occasional bullet overhead, George found the remains of a crossroads just below the 150-metre contour on his map. He struck out to the right towards the next crossroads known as the 'Three Trees', a few hundred metres to the south.

He found the remains of the meandering OG 1 Trench, battered almost to the status of a ditch. It was filled with rubbish: torn groundsheets, mess tins, helmets, rifles and the occasional bloated and twisted corpse in tattered field grey. Fat rats scuttled away from blackened outstretched dead hands. Flies gathered on the faces of the dead. The smell of putre-faction mixed with the acid stench of cordite and high explosives.

Cautiously the men crossed the remains of OG 2 which were located several yards behind the former German fighting trench. The crack of a rifle grenade launcher from just below the crest of the ridge revealed the whereabouts of the Switch Line. It curved parallel to the former German trenches and, although recently completed, was deep and well reinforced.

From the flimsy shelter of OG 2 George could see what needed doing. Munster Alley, a former German communication trench, ran from the end of the former German Pozières Trench, the captured front-line trench that circled round the west side of the village, straight towards the Switch Line at right angles to it. It needed clearing of the enemy so that the Durhams and the Australians could advance on the Switch Line and take it. The only way to do this was to bomb the occupants out of it with supporting rifle and Lewis-gun fire. It was an exposed position at great risk from enemy artillery and infantry attack.

The only answer was boldness. George detailed Noel to direct covering fire from the company and from OG 2 while he checked all available Mills bombs. With two haversacks of bombs slung from his shoulders he checked his revolver and set off into the mouth of Munster Alley with his bombing platoon. Jumping nimbly in and out of the shallow trench he soon saw the movement of men in field grey and coal scuttle helmets. A detached part of George's mind realised that such a close sight of the enemy was unusual. He threw the first bomb straight at the startled faces of the enemy in front of him. Not waiting for the shattering roar he threw two more in quick succession. His men behind him were doing likewise from both sides of the collapsing trench. Rifle fire was being directed into the exposed enemy position as German soldiers ran up the trench towards the Switch Line.

The Germans must have suspected that something was happening close to their line. An artillery barrage straddled Munster Alley and white hot shrapnel and shell fragments flew in every direction. George heard the sizzle of cooling steel in the wet earth around him as he ran. Men fell around him. He waved his bombers into the relative cover of the shallow trench and indicated a digging motion. Each man removed the pick or shovel from the man in front of him and started to dig in, deepening what remained of Munster Alley and throwing the wet clay up on to the edges. As an officer, George was not required to dig at all but he bent to the task of shovelling soil from the trench floor. He could imagine what his men would think of him if he sat down to direct operations while they sweated to improve their chances of survival.

With his tunic draped over his rifle George bent to the task of loosening and removing wet clay. The occasional flint fell out of the growing pile, usually on to his feet. Deafened by the shell fire he worked on with his men on either side, grunting and sweating in the murky drizzle.

A particularly loud explosion rocked the trench as George felt a fiery pain in his left shoulder. Blood dripped on to his hand. He cursed volubly and put down his shovel, picked up his rifle and jacket, and stumbled along the trench to find medical aid. The pain in his shoulder was not so bad. George wondered if there was any hot metal in the wound.

He soon found the medic, who stripped off George's ragged shirt. It was soaked with blood, sweat and mud. The lance corporal probed the wound as George gritted his teeth. He pronounced that there was no metal in the wound and washed it out as best he could. Then he bound up George's shoulder and threw him a spare shirt to put on.

George went straight back to work in the trench. The pain was not too bad and the work had to be done. The regular swing of the shovel tweaked at the wound, which George had been told was a tear rather than a deep puncture wound. It would certainly not keep him out of action. Now George could say that he had been wounded and was glad that it hadn't ruined his good service tunic.

The digging of the trench continued, with men changing regularly from excavating to guarding. Soon it was over seventy feet long and stopped at a blockage made of baulks of timber, sandbags and the remains of an ammunition limber. George posted a strong guard at the end of the trench to make sure that the Germans did not have the presence of mind to mount an attack on the new position.

George found himself wishing that he could light his pipe and thinking about the attack on Mametz by the Devonshire Regiment on the first day of the battle, 1 July. The attack was one of the few successful actions despite the fact that many men were killed in the valley. A few days after the assault the bodies of the fallen Devons were recovered and buried in the former British front-line trenches. The words 'The Devonshires held this trench, the Devonshires hold it still' were written on a plank that was set into the ground near the two neat rows of graves.

He found himself thinking of a trench as a grave. If a trench became a grave it would have to be firmly in the hands of the Army that dug it. He wondered how many of the brave Durhams would be soon buried in the trench that they had been at such pains to dig.

In the morning the drizzle cleared and George imagined the view. From what he had glimpsed from time to time, he remembered the golden spire of the basilica at Albert with the Virgin and child hanging at an acute angle. The baby Jesus, instead of being held up for all the world to see, still appeared to be in the act of being thrown down into the rubble of the street below.

George also imagined the distant view from the top of the dome of the battlefield. The thick woods on the eastern horizon lay close behind the safe chateau of Querrieu where General Rawlinson lived in luxury attended by servants while planning his 'bite and hold' strategies. Around him were fields and houses, parkland with avenues of trees, deer and cattle. While appreciating the irony of the contrast between billets, George did not envy the general his comfort. He hoped that the pleasant surroundings contributed to clear-headed decisions, workable strategies and plans that would save lives rather than squander them. If he were to be honest with himself, however, George doubted whether the best of surroundings would improve the strategies of most of the obdurate men in charge of the war from the Allied point of view.

Soon the weary men and their officers were relieved and made their cautious way back off the ridge and gradually downhill to safe and restful billets. George's wound was examined and properly dressed and pronounced on the mend. It was never going to be a 'Blighty one' that would send him home away from his company and fellow officers. He was glad of this because he wanted, in some strange, perverse way, to see it through.

He thought of how so much of his life had been fragmentary, uncompleted or strangely unsatisfying. Now here was something that he could see through to its logical conclusion. He had a clear vision of what should happen in the securing of Pozières and the move along the ridge towards the north. George found it hard to think that he had been a composer and a dancer. All that seemed so far in the past. Unless he could properly complete what he was doing he would never be able to return to his music after the war's end.

Chapter Sixteen

1 to 5 August 1916

After a few short days spent in Albert, George and A Company were back up on the ridge. Munster Alley, still the dividing line between the Australian and British Armies, was not yet completely wrested away from the Germans, who had gained back most of the trench. Attacks were planned on Munster Alley and the Switch Line, which would have to be taken before the Allied armies swung to the north to take Mouquet Farm and the German strongpoints at Thiepval.

George had written home to reassure his father and stepmother that, despite the report that he had been wounded, he was fine. In a letter dated 27 July he wrote: 'This morning a small fragment hit me in the back, and made a slight scratch, which I had dressed. This is merely to warn you in case you should see my name in the casualty list! They have a way of reporting even the slightest case.' On 29 July he wrote: 'Back in the billets again after two nights only in the line – nothing much doing. Probably going up again soon. Thanks for the letter!'

As July turned into August the nights were beginning to slightly draw in. Thick fog lay on the top of the Pozières – Bazentin ridge. The fog and the intermittent drizzle muffled the digging of a trench linking Black Watch Alley and the trench leading to Munster Alley.

George had ordered this trench excavated parallel to the Switch Line. It curved towards it in the middle and was dug by sweating men obsessed by the urgency of self-protection. As usual George helped in the physical

work. He had posted half the company to provide guard duty and pro-
tective fire. From time to time he ordered the men to reverse roles but kept
digging himself. Occasionally he checked the all-round defence of the
trench, reassuring nervous sentries with a pat on the back and a quick word.

The trench grew to over 200 yards in length. It would provide a
valuable starting-off point for a forward attack on the Switch Line and
for the taking of the rest of Munster Alley, the partially occupied German
communication trench from OG 2 to the Switch Line. Unfortunately,
artillery barrages from Australian and British batteries fell on the new trench
and communications needed to be restored to stop this happening.
Men were pointlessly killed and wounded trying to re-establish the wires
from the new forward trenches to command headquarters. Life in the
newly named 'Butterworth Trench' was becoming precarious. As a result,
the sentries were doubled and a number of German attacks were repulsed.

The tedious business of holding the trench fell to George and his
company. The weather improved and so did the trench. It was never proof
against shells but held out well against rifle and machine-gun fire and
rifle grenades. Constant vigilance kept the enemy at bay as ground was
gained to the south-east and the attack position consolidated.

Plans were made for an attack on 4 August to clear Munster Alley and
also Torr Trench, which sprang from the former at right angles for a short
distance parallel to OG 2. A bombing party led by George and an infantry
attack under Noel Target would be preceded by a brief artillery barrage
that would cause the enemy to keep their heads down for long enough
to be surprised. On the other hand, the barrage could alert the Germans
to the forthcoming attack.

At five minutes past midnight on 5 August 1916, George and A Company
were keeping watch in Butterworth Trench. Through the darkness the
shuffle and occasional clank of a moving body of men could be heard
approaching. A Geordie voice whispered into George's ear: 'Stand down
your company, sir. Await further orders from the brigadier.'

Men dropped quietly into the trench while George placed his men
further up the trench towards the looped section that connected with
Munster Alley. Here they crouched and waited with a few men on guard

duty. Soon the order came: 'Proceed round the loop with your company and form up there for the attack. Take bombs and tools. Move as quickly as possible.'

George felt a fierce excitement. At last here was a chance to make a difference, to winkle the enemy off the ridge. He checked that the men all had grenades and side arms. A few soldiers had pistols, most had trench knives or sharpened spades. Faces were smeared with clay and soil and hessian helmet covers secured to break up the familiar outlines of the new Brodie helmets. Soon a runner instructed George to begin the attack.

Just before the tense men moved off round the loop trench the whoosh and roar of shells rent the night. The men ducked to the bottom of the trench and lay with their hands over their ears. A few were hit as gouts of earth and flints rose into the air on each side of the trench. A few shells came dangerously close. Stones and shell fragments rattled off helmets.

'Stay put!' George shouted. 'Don't move!'

Most of the company realised that the barrage was coming from just below Pozières and was probably from Australian guns. Movement from the trenches adjacent to their positions near Torr Trench must have been detected and presumed to have been that of the enemy. George sent a runner back to report why the company was unable to advance. Nearby, Brigadier Page-Croft was persuaded by his brigade major to forestall the attack. By now the barrage had reached the company that had relieved George's company in Butterworth Trench. Captain Lincoln, of C Company 10th Northumberland Fusiliers, was able to telephone HQ to report the heavy bombardment.

At 2.20am Lieutenant Clark found that Lieutenant Noel Target had been killed, together with quite a lot of his company, having gone 'over the top' in an infantry attack on Munster Alley. Reinforcements from D Company under Second Lieutenants Sant and Atkinson were then organised by Clark to advance towards Munster Alley.

Much to the relief of the men crouching in Butterworth Trench the barrage was finally ended. The message reached George: 'Send a strong bombing party up Munster Alley to our block.' It was 3.45am.

With George at its head, A Company ran round the loop trench and started throwing bombs once again into Munster Alley in front of them.

They ran like dervishes, throwing and slashing at retreating German soldiers. Those who lay wounded were quickly dispatched because of the threat they presented of shooting or bombing from behind. George had only a brief moment to see that all the wounded were already in a pretty bad way. He registered dead Durhams from Noel's company near Munster Alley. Only a few of his company were hit; he wondered if the recent Allied barrage had managed to disable the German guns behind the Switch Trench.

The frantic scrambled bombing of Munster Alley continued until all visible Germans were either sprawling dead at the bottom of the trench or running out of the range of small-arms fire. It was still very dark despite the eerie light from wobbling parachute flares. The stink of blood and high explosive was everywhere. The occasional crack of a rifle could be heard from near and far.

Much of Munster Alley had been taken. There was still a blockage to be removed before the communication trench joined the Switch Line at right angles. The 'bite' had worked, now it had to be 'held'. Reinforcements were ordered up as the first pale grey streaks of dawn appeared behind the Switch Trench. They arrived in platoons and helped to secure Munster Alley. Torr Trench, at the end of Munster Alley farthest from the Switch Trench, was still invested by German soldiers and had to be cleared before any attempt could be made on the Switch Line.

At a few minutes past 4.00am George felt a hand on his shoulder. It was Brigadier Page-Croft.

'You shouldn't be here, sir. It's too risky.'

'Nonsense, George. The situation is too fluid to rely on runners. I have to see for myself before I decide on where to commit the next company.'

'All right sir, but for goodness' sake keep your head down. Most of the parapets are blown down.'

'I'll be careful George. Well done for all your good work.'

'The men were wonderful. They never hesitated.'

Crouching low the two men set off along the trench, trying not to stumble over the fallen men and scattered kit of both sides. The odd round zipped past but the trench was reasonably quiet. The streaks of dawn had grown to a faint light all around the two men.

'Please keep your head down, sir,' George urged.

Page-Croft grunted as he concentrated on the ground in front of the
Switch Line. It was growing lighter. 'Time to go. Much to do.'

'Goodbye, sir. Do be careful.' It was 4.43am as George watched the
brigadier's disappearing back. 'A good man,' he thought. 'But a trifle
reckless.' From somewhere a cock crowed. George's tired brain registered
the sound as being strange. The crow came again. It was 4.45am in the
growing light.

A single sharp crack came from the direction of the Switch Line as
the first low sunbeam slid over the eastern ridge. George's lifeless body slid
down the side of the trench to sprawl gracelessly at the bottom. A look
of surprise was frozen on his face as a thin stream of blood ran down
from the small hole in his temple just below the sackcloth of his helmet.
His hand relaxed and his pistol dropped on to the clay.

He was found a few minutes later. White-faced men dug a hole in the
side of the trench and placed George into it. His identity tags were cut
off and taken back to HQ. The casualties of 5 August for A Company DLI
were: killed, Lieutenant N.A. Target, Lieutenant G.S. Kaye Butterworth
and four other ranks; wounded: Lieutenant Rees, Lieutenant Batty and
eighteen other ranks; three shell shocked and five missing.

It was another day in the gradual taking of the ridge. As the light of dawn
spread to all corners of the battlefield the Australians held the ruins of
Pozières windmill, the highest point of the Somme battlefield. Enfiladed
from the north, the Switch Line was captured a few days later. In the retal-
iatory German artillery fire the parts of Munster Alley containing the buried
bodies of George and Noel Target were repeatedly pounded until no further trace was visible.

Later in the day on 5 August the 13th Battalion DLI were replaced in
Munster Alley by the 8th Battalion Green Howards, a Yorkshire regiment.
They held the sixty yards of Munster Alley against heavy opposition.
Next day the Green Howards captured another 150 yards of Munster Alley
and secured a foothold at last in Torr Trench. It was here that Private
William Short won the Victoria Cross. He was a bomber and, although
immobilised by a wound in the foot and a shattered leg, lay at the bottom
of Torr Trench preparing bombs for his comrades. He refused to be

evacuated for medical treatment and continued to prime grenades until pain and loss of blood caused him to lose consciousness and die. He was buried in the Contalmaison cemetery.

Back at Albert the 13th Durhams regrouped without two of their most effective and popular officers. Up on the ridge the battle ground on. The heavy clay of the ridge was drenched in the blood of countless Australian and British soldiers. Whole trench systems were obliterated in a blighted and increasingly lunar landscape.

At 161 metres above sea level, the Pozières windmill that had been captured by the Australians on 4 August, provided a clear line of sight towards Mouquet farm and Thiepval to the north. The axis of the battle was now shifting along the ridge. The troublesome Switch Line to the east took many days of heavy fighting before it fell. The second line of German trenches had been finally captured. Behind the ridge a well-prepared third German trench system was sited a couple of kilometres to the east along the ruler-straight Albert to Bapaume road. It would take many weeks of fighting and a partially successful new secret weapon, the tank, to force the Germans back to the almost impenetrable Siegfried Line on lower ground east of the uplands of the Somme.

On 9 August Sir Alexander and Lady Butterworth received a slightly ambiguous telegram from the secretary of the War Office. It read: 'Deeply regret to inform you that Lieut. C S Kaye Butterworth Durham Light Infty was killed in action 5th August presumably this refers to Lieut. G S Kaye Butterworth special enquiries are being made to verify this and result will be immediately sent you on receipt the army council express their sympathy.' The confusion between 'C.'S. and 'G.'S. Kaye Butterworth extended a tiny, cruel ray of hope that lasted no time at all.

There were sincere letters of condolence from George's commanding officer Captain George White, written on 6 and 8 August. Another missive came from him enclosing the purple and white ribbon of George's Military Cross. His citation, dated 7 August, was written by Lieutenant Colonel H. Wilkinson: 'Near Pozieres from 17th to 19th July 1916 commanded the Company, of which his Captain had been wounded, with great ability and coolness. By his energy and total disregard of personal safety, he got his men to accomplish a good piece of work in linking up the front line. I have already brought forward the Officer's name for his work during the period 7th to 10th July, 1916.

Brigadier Page-Croft mentioned in a letter that he would have recommended George for the MC for his work in Munster Alley on the day he was killed.

Despite the view by some that George was awarded the MC three times, this is not the case. Unlike the Victoria Cross, the Military Cross was not awarded posthumously. The bringing forward of George's name 'for his work during the period 7th to 10th July' would have been for a Mention in Dispatches, an award that normally preceded the awarding of a Military Cross. On one of George's two campaign medal ribbons there will be a small bronze oak leaf. George's recommendation for the MC preceded his death. Had he lived after his action in Munster Trench he would undoubtedly have been awarded a bar for his MC.

Page-Croft wrote at length to Sir Alexander and Lady Butterworth. He was distressed at the death of such a fine and promising officer, of whom he was fond. He did not realise that George had been so fine a composer before the war. Sir Alexander, in his turn, had not known what an outstanding Army officer George had been. In his letters home George had given no indication of the action in which he had played such a leading part. Yet pride in his late son would never soften the crushing blow of his sudden and violent death.

As the weary days and weeks drew on, the sharp pain of George's death subsided to a deep, dull ache. Letters of condolence arrived from George's friends. Cecil Sharp wrote from the Hotel Algonquin, New York City, on 5 September. He had been collecting folk songs in the Appalachians with his friend and secretary Maud Karpeles. 'In George's death I have lost one of my best and dearest friends. I was very very fond of him and have no one to take his place in my affections. We had done a lot of work together and our aims were pretty nearly identical.'

Ralph Vaughan Williams wrote from France, in execrable handwriting, on 16 August: 'You know how my wife and I loved and admired him.' His wife, Adeline, had written on 15 August from the family home at 13 Cheyne Walk, London: 'Dear George's father, if my Ralph comes back he will miss him beyond anything I can say.'

Other letters came from, among others, Helen Kennedy, née Karpeles, now Honorary Secretary of the English Folk Dance Society. She wrote from Stratford-upon-Avon where she and her husband, Douglas Kennedy, were taking part in the month-long festival in which George had corresponded that he had, for once, felt truly happy.

Guy Granet, General Manager of the Midland Railway, wrote on 13 August. One of the last of the numerous letters, including one addressed erroneously to 'Sir Alfred', came from Sir Hubert Parry, George's old teacher and friend.

It says a lot about the genuine affection in which George was held that so many of his friends expressed emotions normally uncommunicated by English people who normally kept a tight rein on their feelings. There was something about George's character, a directness, a bluntness, that cut through the normal English reserve, even among people who normally mainly conveyed strong feelings only in their music.

George's estate was worth over £4,000; it included small amounts owed him by the British Army and just over £1 found in his kit. A fund to encourage musicians and the collection of folk songs was set up by his father, in accordance with his wishes. It is ironic that George, at the end of his short life, was finally quite well off.

In 1918 Sir Alexander and Lady Butterworth compiled a book of remembrance, which was circulated among George's family and friends. An oak plaque with the carved names of George and his cousin Hugh was placed on the door of Deerhurst Church. On it was carved the regimental badges of both officers.

Chapter Seventeen

One Hundred Years Later

Today the uplands where the 141 days of the Somme battle was fought have long returned to agriculture. When the French civilians went back to their shattered villages and farms they began the long process of rebuilding. Trenches and shell holes were filled in and ploughing began. Tractors and crawlers with armour plate between the driver and the plough began to turn up the 'iron harvest'. Scrap dealers flourished as thousands of tons of iron, steel, barbed wire, shrapnel balls, elephant iron, helmets and rusting weapons were cleared from the land. There were many casualties from unexploded shells, high explosives, shrapnel and gas. Small boys trudged behind the plough picking up shrapnel to take to the scrap man. Eighty shrapnel balls weighed approximately one kilogram.

Men of all nations continued to die from the effects of wounds, gas and trauma. 'Mutilés de guerre' were given reserved seats on trains, trams and buses. Unemployment was high and malnutrition was rife, particularly in Germany.

As the shattered land began to green over and return to farming, the dedicated men of the Imperial War Graves Commission took over the recovery of soldiers' remains from the Army. Cemeteries were concentrated around former first-aid posts, casualty clearing stations and base hospitals. The men who came home to die of their wounds were given the same gravestones as the men who were buried in France and Belgium.

No distinction was made for rank in the design of these stones. It was the democratisation of death; the normal rigid class distinctions counted for nothing in the cities of the dead. Servicemen and women who died as the result of the war before 31 August 1921 were all given Portland Stone grave markers of a uniform shape and size.

Nearly half the dead of the Somme were never found. Like George and his cousin Hugh in Belgium they have become a less obvious part of the landscape. From time to time human remains are found and occasionally identified and laid to rest in Commonwealth War Grave Commission cemeteries.

During the 1920s the villages of the Somme were rebuilt: Pozières, Martinpuich, Le Sars, Flers, Contalmaison and others. Cellar holes indicated where houses had once stood. When the piles of rubble were removed and used to reconstruct roads and tracks, houses were rebuilt, like their predecessors, in brick. Some houses were erected farther back from the roads; some replaced the flimsy prefabs that were thrown up immediately after the end of the war. Churches were rebuilt, town halls combined with schools and once more proudly flew the tricolor.

Charabancs containing the wives and families of soldiers who fought in the war drove the circuit of the battlefields, paying their respects to the dead who lay below their white wooden crosses. The tyre manufacturer Michelin produced guides to the battlefield with engraved illustrations of the main features.

Woods were replanted and fences rebuilt, often using rails from the former narrow-gauge system that crossed the battlefield. Screw pickets were used as fence posts and pigs lived in former concrete bunkers.

Today the changes and remains are more subtle than on many former battlefields. There are very few ruins. Large fields of maize, wheat and sugar beet separate quiet little villages. Woods and copses flourish on the clay soil and chalk of hilltops and slopes. From the top of the ridge at Pozières there is an almost 360° view off the dome of the Somme uplands. On the far western horizon are the woods behind the Château de Querrieu where Rawlinson directed the attacks in parts of the battle. The golden Virgin and Child glints vertically in the sun from the middle of the small town of Albert. To the north, along the ridge, looms the huge brick and stone arch of Lutyens' monument at Thiepval and its softening woods. On the inside of one of the side arches can be found the engraved names of Lieutenant George Sainton Kaye Butterworth, MC, and Lieutenant Noel Target, MC.

Leaving the pleasant but unremarkable town of Albert, a roundabout marks the bottom of the gradual ascent up the arrow-straight Roman road to Bapaume. Very soon the Bapaume Post Cemetery is seen on the right, opposite the last buildings of a modern industrial estate.

The road rises up a gentle, bare hill. On the right is Tara Hill, on the left is Usna Hill, both killing grounds of Tyneside Scottish and Irish soldiers on the first day of the battle. After a dip in the road the village of La Boisselle straddles the road. A small sign with a blood-red poppy shows where the British front line was positioned on the western edge of the village on 1 July 1916. A turning to the right leads past a smaller mine crater to the enormous Lochnagar Crater where traces of the German front line can be found beside the road. Shell holes, now softened by turf, pock the ground beside the walkway around the crater.

Leaving La Boisselle on the Roman road, the nearby village of Ovillers can be seen in a shallow valley to the north. A large cemetery lies to the west. In it can be found the grave of Private Strickland, one of George's men of the 13th Battalion, Durham Light Infantry.

As the road climbs gently towards Pozières the shallow valleys on each side are Sausage Valley to the south and Mash Valley to the north. The view to the south reveals woods and the spire of Contalmaison Church. The country here is generally more broken than the downland to the north. This is the landscape that George and his men bombed, shot and dug their way through up to Pozières Ridge. It is deceptive; the narrow roads tend to follow the contours of the hills, curving between areas of woodland and steep little winding valleys.

Just before the village of Pozières is a large colonnaded cemetery on the left with its ordered graves and enclosing wall with the names of the missing inscribed in their regiments. There are many graves of Australian soldiers here to remind us that the capture of Pozières was a mainly Australian feat of arms. On the edge of the village is the massive Australian monument and the remains of the German Gibraltar Redoubt, a hole in the ground with huge chunks of concrete and an intact staircase leading down into the depths.

Pozières, like la Boisselle, is bisected by the Bapaume road. It has, on the right, 'Le Tommy' café, which caters for tourists, researchers and locals. It is something of a museum, changing its theme from time to time. In the quiet courtyard at the back is an incredible number of rusty shells, broken rifles and bayonets, and a museum with trenches through a door behind. Like the village of Pozières the cafe is a plain, honest place. What you see is what you get.

At the eastern edge of the village a sign indicates a right-hand turn to Bazentin. A smaller sign shows that 'Butterworth Farm' lies that way too. Turn on to the D73, a minor road, then after 100 metres, turn to the left marked as 'Le Chemin de Butterworth'. On the right is an orchard, opposite a short driveway to a newly built gite called Butterworth Farm. Outside the gîte is a collection of the usual shells and screw pickets. There is also a German steel helmet and lengths of narrow-gauge rail. Inside the modern and very comfortable hostelry there are trench maps on the wall and a number of photographs of George on the walls. There is a panoramic photograph of the lunar wartime landscape around Pozières in 1916 and an extensive library of books about George and his music.

The gîte was built by Monsieur Bernard Delattre and his wife Marie. Monsieur Delattre is the mayor of Pozières and is a great lover of George's music. He is an ex-marine engineer and Paris police detective. His grandparents owned the farmland nearby where George was killed. Early in the Great War Monsieur Delattre's grandmother asked a German soldier what on earth they were doing on her farm. The soldier looked sadly at her. 'I really have no idea,' he politely replied.

Walking back to the entrance to Le Chemin de Butterworth this author was told that the place where George was killed was located 330 metres across the fields from the recent Butterworth monument erected by the Commonwealth War Graves Commission. A short walk up the road past a grain silo brought me to a slight curve in the road. Beside the road is a metal CQ post that has a barcode on its angled top. Accessible by smartphone, it tells about Private Short, VC, who died a few yards away in Torr Trench and George, whose death site is a few yards further on.

At the apex of the slight curve in the road there was once a crossroads.
Today only the western track remains across the fields. The eastern track
bisected the loop that led from Butterworth Trench to Munster Alley.
The spot where George died and near where his scattered remains still
lie is about twenty metres into the field.

There is no sign today of the extensive trench systems, just flattish
fields and crops. From the place where George was killed one can see a
distant crossroads with a line of trees and a house. This marks the other
end of Butterworth Trench at the place shown as 'Three Trees' on the trench
maps of 1916.

There is a lingering sadness on this part of the ridge a few hundred
metres from the edge of Pozières. Whether it is actual or by association
is open to question. George never reached Pozières. He died in the parish
of Contalmaison a few hundred metres from the point on the ridge where
the departement of Somme ends and Pas de Calais begins. At that point
Picardie becomes Artois, the only difference being that a slight slope
upwards becomes a slight slope downwards.

Turning round to explore the western track of the defunct crossroads
I found two unexploded shells by the side of the track awaiting collection.
They were both British, 9lb and 18lb high-explosive shells. Perhaps they
were part of the 'friendly fire' that bloodily hampered George's progress
towards Munster Alley. Farther along the track I found part of an exploded German shell's brass nose cone.

Back on the edge of Pozières I found that Le Chemin de Butterworth
had once been the trackbed of a narrow-gauge railway that had been built
before the Great War to haul sugar beet and other agricultural products
to the mills. A walk along this track crossed the former sites of the three
German trenches: OG 1, OG 2 and the notorious Switch Line. No trace of
these trenches can be found in the summer. Aerial photographs taken
in the winter show faint chalky marks on the soil where the trenches
once were.

Once over the ridge the track descends past a line of tall trees to become
a metalled farm road leading to the village of Martinpuich. While walking on this track you realise that the sky is a huge part of the Somme
landscape. Exploring a rough track going south from the metalled road

I soon dug up a brass nose cone from a 9lb British shell, marked, as expected, with the year 1916.

Martinpuich is a long village with a number of farms off the main street. It took the Allied armies another five weeks to fight their way from Pozières to Martinpuich. At the Pozières end of Martinpuich is a very tidy dairy farm with an orchard on the right-hand side of the road. On the far side of the orchard, neatly fenced off from it by screw pickets to make it accessible to the public, is a German concrete bunker surrounded by a strip of mown grass. Its humped structure has a doorway to the east, a loophole to the north and the marks of shrapnel and high-explosive shells on the west side, an understated microcosm of the course of the war.

Back over the crest of the ridge at Pozières the Roman road crests the ridge at the site of its windmill just east of the village. The windmill ruins are an Australian monument. Behind it on a round water tank is the painting of an Australian soldier, a 'Digger' in a slouch hat, and a list of the six men who won the VC at Pozières as well as an officer who was awarded a VC at Gallipoli and fought at Pozières. Across the road from the windmill is the Tank Monument. After Pozières was wrested from the Germans a new phase of the battle began a little way down the road. Tanks were used for the first time at the nearby villages of Flers and Courcelette, with mixed success. But this is to get ahead of the phase of the war that George knew.

Back in Pozières at around the time that the combine harvesters are moving over the fields cutting the wheat, an annual event has taken place for the last few years. It is a commemoration of the death of George Butterworth and a celebration of his life.

On the first Sunday morning after 5 August, almost every year, many people gather at the entrance to Le Chemin de Butterworth to hear speeches and music. A piper in full military uniform plays laments, a brass ensemble from Amiens perform popular songs from the Great War, veterans of the Second World War and the Resistance parade with medals under banners and a French morris side dances in the road. The event is organised by the mayors of Pozières and Contalmaison.

The most important part of the ceremony is a speech by George's first cousin Hugh Montagu Butterworth. He is a dignified man in his middle eighties, the half-brother of Hugh Montagu Butterworth, George's first cousin, who was killed at Hooge, near Ypres, in 1915. A retired solicitor from North Devon, he shares George's sense of humour and awareness of the ridiculous.

He made an amused face and laughed when listening to the speech of introduction in French, which referred to his 'advanced age'. He is an enthusiastic man with a very sharp mind and an excellent memory. When I told him that I was writing a biography of his cousin he looked at me quizzically. He seemed quite satisfied with my account that I was writing about the man and his military experiences rather than analysing his music. Had he not been happy with my explanation I am quite sure that he would have let me know in a few quiet words that would have put me firmly and kindly in my place.

Hugh Butterworth has done a lot to quietly bring both George and his brother Hugh into the public eye. He recently edited his brother's letters from the front to his friends in New Zealand. The book entitled *Blood and Iron*, with an introduction by Hugh, is a very valuable window into his brother's experience as an infantry officer in some intense action before his tragic death. His letters hold nothing back. Because he was writing to friends rather than worried parents he was able to express all the boredom, fear and exhilaration of close-quarter combat.

Nearly all the Butterworth family come and stay at Butterworth Farm for the commemoration each early August. Shaunagh and her husband Fred Perity, their sons Jesse and Ben are there keeping a fond eye on their Uncle Hugh. Staying nearby are John Goldsmith and his wife Anthea Ionides, great-granddaughter of Dorothea. She recently gave a box of papers to the Bodleian Library in Oxford. Still unclassified, they are a valuable insight into her great-grandmother Dorothea who became Sir Alexander's second wife and her great-grandfather Alfred Mavor who, in Sir Alexander's letter to George, was 'a man who proved to be already a confirmed drunkard' by the time he married the eighteen-year-old Dorothea.

Sir Alexander and Dorothea Butterworth had a long and happy marriage despite Dorothea's semi-invalid state. She and George soon became very fond of each other and corresponded frequently up to the time of George's death. She sent him books and magazines and comforts in the trenches. He, in his turn, did not reveal to her the full horror of what he was experiencing during his brief but intense time in the war. She was, according to Hugh, a 'strong, independently minded lady'.

Hugh also remembers Sir Alexander, or 'Uncle Alick' as he calls him, as a wonderful man – generous, humane and dedicated to the greater good of mankind. Hugh's link to George's father and stepmother are particularly valuable and important. His observations provide an insight into George's family and upbringing. One cannot help but wonder how different George would have been had he grown up with brothers or sisters.

The Pozières annual commemorations provide a link to George, as 'some corner of a foreign field' tied to the England of a hundred years ago. I can almost hear George snorting disparagingly at the reference to Rupert Brooke, a poet whom he initially liked but with whom he soon became disenchanted.

If we ask ourselves why George Butterworth is so fondly remembered today all we need to do to answer the question is to consider his music. He composed around three hours of choral and orchestral music, which all endure today. The rest, by his own choice, is lost. There is enough extant to show the perfection of his work, the range and the mature appropriateness of his settings.

A.E. Housman was grudging in his praise of any musical settings of his poems. There were many composers who set them to music: Vaughan Williams, Butterworth, Gurney, Finzi and many more. Housman tacitly approved of George's settings more than most others, considering their tone and feeling to be most like what he intended.

Housman and George shared a tension in their lives. Housman's was caused by the loss of Moses Jackson, the love of his life who could never return Housman's affection and who moved away to India and an early death in Canada. George's tension was the intense self-criticism caused by the perfectionism that ruled his musical life as well as his inability to find a means of making a steady living that suited him before joining the Army. When George said 'the war gave me something to do' he was being entirely serious. We may mistake the apparent flippancy of his remark but to do so would be to misunderstand George's capacity for self-knowledge.

In the Army, particularly as an infantry officer, George found a vocation quite apart from his composition. He found men whose lives and welfare depended on his decisions and capacity for empathy and decisive action. He was able to overcome his shyness and use his bluntness to good effect. The Army suited him. He fitted in far better than he had adapted to writing criticism and to teaching. He was undoubtedly good at both these professions but the Army gave him results in the same way that morris dancing did. You had to get it right. There was one chance and immense satisfaction if you succeeded.

The few photographs of George show two sides of his character. In most images he looks serious, a man hiding behind hair and a moustache. One gets the impression that he usually didn't want to be photographed and resolved to give little away. There are a few photographs of George in a more casual mood. The best shows him smoking his pipe with a twinkle in his eye. His collar is up around the back of his neck and his rumpled white shirt somewhat bunched up. The picture was taken during the month-long Folk Dance Festival at Stratford-upon-Avon in August 1914. There is a similar photograph of George in the back row of a group of dancers, holding his pipe, taken a few minutes before or after the pipe-smoking picture. In both images George looks completely happy. He had, for a few weeks, found his place in the world.

There are the two Georges apparent in the 1912 Kinora film of morris and folk dancing at Kelmscott. There is the dark, intense, almost expressionless George vigorously and skilfully demonstrating a number of morris dances. There is also a more relaxed George participating in a country dance and colliding with Cecil Sharp. In the quick smile of amusement is the real, more secret George, the George whose incisive sense of humour comes across in some of his letters and remarks to friends.

There is no authenticated photograph of George in the Army. There is an undated group photograph of officers of the Durham Light Infantry that contains an officer who looks like George. He is standing, like his fellow officers, smart and upright with his service cap pulled down. He has a thick moustache but his ears stick out in a way that George's never did and the shape of his face is subtly different. Unfortunately it doesn't appear to be George. Some writers have blurred the photograph, a tacit admittance that they were not quite sure if the image was of George or not.

The questions will always remain. Would George have been able to return to composition? Would he have come back to an England so changed by the war to be unrecognisable to him? With the encouragement of his friends, could he have settled down to make the best of the hollowness of 'the land fit for heroes'?

We can imagine him after the war, now in his middle-thirties, his abundant hair and luxuriant moustache beginning to be slightly streaked with grey. Perhaps he would have taken the time to go back to Deerhurst, to walk up Bredon Hill and admire the panoramic view and listen to the larks, to return to the north country and to Oxfordshire. Perhaps he would have talked long and deeply with his father, with Ralph Vaughan Williams and with other friends. Perhaps he would have eventually been able to compose music recollecting an England that had survived all that had been thrown at it in the last few years. Perhaps we should leave him there.

Acknowledgements

There are so many people to thank. In chronological order I thank Steve Darlow, my publisher and friend, who asked me to write this biography of a remarkable man. He published my book on my grandfather's experiences in both world wars a few years ago, read my biography of the Cornish poet Charles Causley, and took a risk. Let's hope his ball went through the hoop!

Great thanks are also due to my wife Kathi who is the most uncanny finder of battlefield artefacts that I know. She never tires of visiting Commonwealth War Grave Commission cemeteries or of researching fallen soldiers.

Next I owe a great debt to Hugh Montagu Butterworth, whose quiet encouragement and friendship have been so vital to the writing of this book. His incisive advice and close reading of the manuscript have put me right on many occasions.

Thank you to John and Anthea Ionides Goldsmith, who gave me valuable information and material as well as riotous evenings in French restaurants and hotels.

Shaunagh and Fred Perity and their two sons have been very encouraging and welcoming and I thank them for their friendship.

Monsieur and Madame Bernard Delattre have helped me a lot with topographical and historic details. Their organisation of the George Butterworth reunion and vision of the future of Pozières is wonderful.

I should very much like to thank the staff of Radley College for making my wife and I so welcome when we came to the excellent concert of George Butterworth's music in May 2016. The music was beautifully performed and the talks that took place on the following morning very informative.

My gratitude to John Bridcutt, who introduced the pieces of George's music and who came especially to the commemoration day in Pozières. Maybe one day I'll succeed in persuading him to make a documentary film about George Butterworth.

Thank you to the helpful staff at the Bodleian Library in Oxford where I spent half a day reading through the three boxes of material relating to George's short life.

My appreciation goes to Liz Chandler, our very capable church organist who played for me a composition from a manuscript of Butterworth's music sent to me by Hugh Butterworth.

Many thanks to Jennie and John Knight at the Silent Picket in Martinpuich, Pas de Calais, whose hospitality and help went well beyond the call of duty.

And thank you to all my friends who love George's music and can whistle or even sing snatches of George's songs from memory.

Bibliography

George Butterworth
Barlow, Michael. *Whom the Gods Love.* London: Toccata Press, 1997.
Copley, Ian A. *George Butterworth.* London: Thames Publishing, 1985.
Murphy, Anthony. *Banks of Green Willow: The Life and Times of George Butterworth.* Malvern: Cappella Archive, 1988.
Sharp, Cecil James; Butterworth, George; Karpeles, Maud. *The Country Dance Book (Volume – Pt.1).* London: Novello, 1909.
Smith, Wayne. *George Butterworth Memorial Volume, Centenary Edition.* Oxford and Shrewsbury: Youcaxton Publications, 2015.

World War One.
Buchan, John. *The Battle of the Somme: The First and Second Phase.* London: Endeavour, 2016.
Ed. Cooksley, John. *Blood and Iron: Letters from the Western Front. Hugh Montagu Butterworth.* Barnsley: Pen and Sword, 2011.
Crouch, Lionel William. *Duty and Service: Letters from the Front.* London: Forgotten Books, 2015.
Hart, Peter. *The Somme.* London: Weidenfeld and Nicolson, 2005.
Keech, Graham. *Battleground Somme, Pozieres.* Barnsley: Pen and Sword, 2015.
Lewis-Stempel, John. *Six Weeks: The Short and Gallant Life of the British Officer in the First World War.* London: Orion, 2011.
Meeres, Charles. *I Survived the Somme: The Secret Diary of a Tommy.* Stroud: Amberley, 2013.
Sebag-Montefiore, Hugh. *Somme: Into the Breach.* London: Penguin Viking, 2016.

Contemporaries.
Foss, Hubert. *Ralph Vaughan Williams.* London: Harrap, 1950.
Hurd, Michael. *The Ordeal of Ivor Gurney.* Oxford: Oxford University Press, 1984.
Parker, Peter. *Housman Country: Into the Heart of England.* London: Little, Brown, 2016.
Vaughan Williams, Ursula. *RVW: A Biography of Ralph Vaughan Williams.* Oxford: Oxford University Press, 1988.

Index

123

1/4th Gloucesters 128
1/5th Gloucesters 128–129
1/6th Gloucesters 128
144th Brigade 128
145th Brigade 128
1st and 4th Ox and Bucks Light Infantry 128–129
1st Corps 128
1st Division (Australian) 128
23rd Division 77
2nd Division (Australian) 128
3rd Corps 128
48th Division 128
68th Brigade 99

A

Adeline, Vaughan Williams 146
Albert 105–107,126,133,135,139,140,145,149
Aldershot 64–65,67,74–76
Allen, Hugh 34,50,57
Allen, John 81
Alliston, Private 125
Ardingly 30
Armentiéres 78–79,87
Ashby, Colonel 74

Atkinson, Second Lieutenant 142
Aysgarth 7,10,12,14,23,38

B

Bailiff Wood 112–113,116,135
Ball, Private 122
Bapaume 105–106,135,150
Barker, Harley Granville 49
Barnet, Major 66
Batty, Lieutenant 144
Bax, Alexander 52
Bax, Arnold 98
Bayswater 47,54
Bazentin 140
Beaumont Hamel 112
Bécourt Wood 109,112–113,118,125
Bellewaarde 80–81
Biddulph, Major 74
Birdwood, William 128
Birmingham 61,62,63
Bishop of Lincoln 3
Bishop of Liverpool 26
Bishop's Cleeve 44
Blomfield, Reginald 81
Bodleian Library 154
Bodmin 61,62,64,65,67
Booker, R.P.L. 21,23

Boulogne 88–89,94,103
Boult, Adrian 51,52
Bramshott 75–78
Bredon Hill 1,50,53,157
Breitkopf & Hartel 56
Brooke, Rupert 155
Brookshank, G. 23
Brown, P.A. 61–62,69,71,86–87,96
Bullswater Camp 70,73–76
Busch, Fritz 56
Butterworth, Alexander 1–3,5,6,15–16,
18,22–24,34,51,54–57,60,91–93,103,
145–147,155
Butterworth, George (uncle) 15
Butterworth, Hugh 10–11,14,16–17,
21,28–29,35,37,76–77,80–82,91,147,149
Butterworth, Hugh Montagu 154–155
Butterworth, Irene 76
Butterworth, Reverend George 2–4,29

C

Callow, John 7
Cambridge 7
Carr, Private 122
Charing Cross 62
Chavasse, Noel 26
Chelsea 39,47,51
Christchurch 99
Churchill, Winston 99
Churchward, Mr 62
Clark, Lieutenant 119,123,133,142
Coat 65
Colles, H.C. 37
Contalmaison 105,109,113,115,117,
120,123–124,126–127,135–136,149–150,
152–153
Courcelette 153
Cox & Co 70

D

Dale, Private 118
Deerhurst 1,3–4,15,29,43,147,157
Delattre, Bernard 151

Delattre, Marie 151
Devonport 62
Devonshire regiment 138
Dover 90
Duke of Cornwall's Light Infantry
60–63,68–70,74
Dunhill, Thomas 21
Durham 96
Durham Light Infantry 68,71,75,82,
86–87,102,112–115,131–132,135–136,
143–145,150,156

E

Ealing 17
Edinburgh 22
Edmunds, Sergeant 66
Elgar, Edward 32,41,47,51
Ellis, Bevis 52
Ellis, F.B. 61,65,69,71
Ellis, R.A. 61,67,69,71
English Folk Dance Society 47
Esperance Working Girls' Club 47
Eton 7,13–21,23

F

Ferdinand, Archduke Franz 56
Ferdinand, Sophia 56
Finzi 155
Flers 149,153
Folk Song Society 38
Frenvillers 132,133
Fuller-Maitland, J.A. 37

G

Gallipoli 99,153
Gloucester VIII,IX,43,94
Gloucestershire Regiment 94
Goldsmith, John 154
Gough, Hubert 128
Grady, Stephen IX
Granet, Guy 147
Green Howards 144

Green, Private   118
Guildford   77
Gurney, Ivor   VIII,45,53,94,109,155

H

Haig, Field Marshal   106
Hales, Thomas   7
Hammond, Lieutenant   68
Hampstead   54,88,90,103,126
Handsworth   63
Hanwell   17
Haselmere   77
Hollingshead, Private   118
Hooge   154
Horse Guard's Parade   62
Housman, A.E.   VIII,38–39,42,46,
   50–51,53,55,127,155
Howells, Herbert   VIII,45

I

Ionides, Anthea   154
Isle of Wight   20
Iver Heath   17

J

Jackson, Moses   155

K

Karpeles, Helen   40–43,47–49,147
Karpeles, Maud   40–43,47–49,146
Keeling, F.H.   61,66,68,70
Kelmscott   48–49,156
Kemble   43
Kennedy, Douglas   43,47,147
Kenny, Thomas   87,96
King's Cross   16,25

L

La Boiselle   105,112,151
La Houssoie   87

Le Sars   149
Leeds   51
Leipzig   56
Ley, Henry   57
Lincoln, Captain   142
Lloyd, C.H.   23
Lloyd, Charles Harford   21
Lochnager Crater   113
London   25,27,29,33,
   37–39,43,45,47,52,60–63,70–71,80,88,90,
   103,106,146
London Symphony Orchestra   51
Loos   80,82,87
Lowry, Mr   17–18
Lyons, Ponsonby   129

M

Malplaquet   74–75
Malvern   1
Mametz   138
Margate   61
Marlborough   14,16–17
Martinpuich   105,112,129,136,149,152–153
Mary Neal   47
Mavor, Alfred   154
Mavor, Dorothea   54,56–57,60,
   85,91–93,145–147
McInnes, Campbell   51
Menin Gate   81
Millencourt   106–107
Morris, R.O.   60–61,67,69,71,74
Morris, William   49
Mouquet Farm   112,127,136,140,14
5

N

Nauheim   56
New York   146
Nikisch, Arthur   51
Noble, Private   122
Northumberland Fusiliers   71,142

O

Ovens, General   68–69,74

Ovillers 129
Oxford 7,19–20,22,24–29,33, 35–36,38,50,57,61,154
Oxford Folk Dance Society 47

P

Paddington 5, 17,25,62
Page-Croft, Henry 99,101,142–144,146
Paris 46,75,106,151
Parratt, Sir Walter 46
Parry, Sir Hubert 46,92,147
Pascoe, Sergeant 64
Pentland Hills 22
Perity, Ben 154
Perity, Fred 154
Perity, Jesse 154
Perity, Shaunagh 154
Perth 22
Peterborough 16
Pirbright 69,70
Plymouth 62
Poziéres 105,112–113,117, 120,127–128,131–134,136,139–140,142, 144–145,149–153,155
Princip, Gavrilo 56
Pulford, Corporal 125
Purcell, Henry 61
Purvis, Lance Sergeant 125

Q

Querrieu 139,149

R

Radley 37–39,50
Railway Wood 81
Ravel 46
Rawlinson, General 139
Rees, Lieutenant 144
Rifle Brigade 76,80
Riseholme 5
Royal Army Medical Corps 93
Royal Berkshires 129
Royal College of Music 27,39,41–42,45–46
Royal Munster Fusiliers 130

S

Sailly-sur-le-Lys 79
Saint-Julien 87
Sant, Second Lieutenant 142
Sassoon, Siegfried 108
Savoy Theatre 49
Scotland Yard 60,61
Scott, Lance Corporal 125
Sharp, Cecil 33–34,38–42,45, 47–49,60,146,156
Shelley 46
Short, Private 151
Short, William 144
Slough 17
Southall 17
Southwold 46
St Andrew's Hall 47
St Lawrence's Mental Hospital 64
St Peter's College 37
Stratford-upon-Avon 47–48,60,110,147
Strickland, Private 125,150
Swindon 16–17,28

T

Target, Lieutenant Noel 98–99,103–104, 107–108,110,113–114,117–120,123,125, 127–128,132–133,136–137,141–144,150
Taunton 108
Tel-el-Kebir 74
Tewkesbury 1
Thiepval 112,127,133,140,145,150
Thirsk 7
Thomas, Edward 42,45
Thomas, Helen 42
Todd, Private 125
Toye, E.G. 61,66,68,70
Toye, Geoffrey 51
Trinity College 24,26

V

Vaughan Williams, Ralph VIII,26–31 33–34,38–39,43–47,51–53,56–57,61,

93,103,109,146,155,157

Verdun   95,97,101,111
Victoria Station   90
Villiers-Stuart, Charles   76,80
Vowles, Captain   129

W

Walker, H.B.   128
Walton, Private   122
Wanganui   35,76,81
Watts   65
Watts Common   65,67,69,76
Wearmouth, Private   125
Welwyn Garden City   57
West Kirby   51
White, Captain   87,96,114,145
Wiesbaden   56
Wilkinson, H.   145
Winchcombe   44
Woking   68
Wood, Charles   46
Woodhead, R.C.   61,66,69,71
Wright, Michael   IX

Y

York   1–2,5,7,10–11,14–17,23,25,34–35,39
Ypres   80–81,87,154